Tiramisu Amore r

Varinia Cappelletti & Edoardo Cecotto

Tiramisu Amore Mio

Tiramisù Amore Mio™
(Tiramisu My Love)
30 Easy New Creative Recipies

Copyright © 2012 by Varinia Cappelletti and Edoardo Cecotto
All rights reserved. No part of this publication (included the interactive part) may be reproduced, distributed, or transmitted in any form or by any means, including photocopying, recording, or other electronic or mechanical methods, without the prior written permission of the publisher, except in the case of brief quotations embodied in critical reviews and certain other noncommercial uses permitted by copyright law. For permission requests, write to the authors, addressed "Attention: Permissions Coordinator," at the address below.

White Lily LLC
332 Bleecker St. F4#
10014 NY, New York
www.whitelilyusa.com
customer@whitelilyusa.com

Ordering Information:
Quantity sales. Special discounts are available on quantity purchases by corporations, associations, and others. For details, contact the authors at the address above.

First Edition
2012

Authors:
Varinia Cappelletti
Edoardo Cecotto

Editorial Director: Varinia Cappelletti, Edoardo Cecotto
Design Director: Varinia Cappelletti, Edoardo Cecotto
Cover Design: Edoardo Cecotto
Cover art and illustrations: Edoardo Cecotto
Photograph: Edoardo Cecotto
Recipe development: Varinia Cappelletti

A mamma Carla e papà Rinaldo

A mamma Mariagrazia e papà Giorgio
A nonna Elisa
A Marco e Celestelisa

Our thanks to everybody that have supported us.
In alphabetical order:

Justin and Vanessa Daigle for hospitality, help, for have trust in our work. They are great friends.
Tom Kornrumpf and Jan Olson for the great hospitality, the great affection and generosity.
Holly LeDu for give us the oportunity to our first public presence in San Francisco.
MaryKey and Ron Mauro for give us the oportunity and for follow our dinners...any time!
Kim Minarovich like our first Agent. For great hospitality, good job and friendly.
Patti e Franck Ralko for trust in our job, hospitality and affection.
Carol, Mike and Kattni Rembor for immense love!
Kattni Rembor for the great suggestion and availability.
Ginger Trevarrow for wonderfull locations and for help us to grow up.

Thanks, also to our friends:
Judit Bishop, Tom Rushfeldt and Brenda Fake, Mindy and Mary Ellen Fiddler, Ben Goodman and Javier, Cristina Van Patten and Brian Kerchner, Roberta Maccioni, Glenn and Othis Raynolds.

Introduction

Tiramisu Amore mio
Tiramisu My love

We pay tribute to the most well known dessert in the world.
In this book we will introduce you to 30 recipes that are simple, yet impressive, that you can make for yourself or for company.

We tried to make the recipes using easily available ingredients.
You'll find QR codes for every recipe that allow you to quickly save the shopping list on your device, as well as connect to our website where you'll find extra content including videos, variations on recipes and more!

And, now on to a great time!

INDEX

6	WHY IS THIS MORE THAN A COOKBOOK?
7	THE ORIGIN, THE HISTORY OF THE MOST POPULAR ITALIAN DESSERT
8	ORIGINAL RECIPE
10	INGREDIENTS
12	Eggs
12	Mascarpone
12	Coffee
12	Ladyfingers and sponge cake
13	Ricotta
13	Spirits
14	TOOLS
16	EXTRA RECIPES
18	Sponge cake
19	Landyfingers
20	HOW TO MAKE SYRUP
20	Any type of berries (blueberries, strawberries, raspberries)
21	Orange syrup
21	Mint syrup
22	HOW TO MAKE BASIC CREAM
23	HOW TO MAKE CHOCOLATE CREAM
23	HOW TO MAKE THE FRUITS CREAM
24	RECIPES
28	Tiramisù with cinnamon and coffee
30	Double chocolate tiramisù
32	Chocolate and caramelized orange tiramisù
34	Tiramisù cinnamon and meringue
36	Tiramisù chocolate and pistachio
38	Tiramisù with nougat and cinnamon
40	Chocolate and granola tiramisù
42	Cappuccino tiramisù
44	Tiramisù vanilla, cinnamon and warm chocolate
46	Chocolate and mint tiramisù
48	Tiramisù with crunchy caramel

50	TIRAMISU RECIPES WITH ALCOHOL
52	Tiramisù chocolate, cherries and rum
54	Irish coffee tiramisù
56	Whisky cream tiramisù
58	Tiramisù chocolate, coffee and rum
60	Tiramisù toffee cream, pear and amaretto
62	TIRAMISU WITH FRUITS
64	Banana tiramisù
66	Raspberries and honey tiramisù
68	Tiramisù with "mixed barries"
70	Tiramisù with fresh strawberries
72	Tiramisù with fresh cherries
74	Tiramisù with fresh orange and chocolate
76	Tiramisù with blueberries and wafers
78	Tiramisù vanilla, chocolate and strawberries
80	Coconut tiramisù
82	TIRAMISU WITH FRUITS AND ALCOHOL
84	Limoncello tiramisù
86	Tiramisù with dried fruits and cointreau
88	Tiramisù piñacolada
90	SPECIAL RECIPES
92	Tiramisù with stout beer
94	Chocolate and red chili tiramisù

Tiramisu Amore Mio

Why is this more than a cookbook?

This is not only a book. It goes beyond! Through it you'll have access to **photos, videos updates** and **variations on recipes**.

You can read the QR Code or follow the link at the bottom of the page.

With this code, you'll have the ability to access more information from any smartphone, tablet or computer. There is software free for **iPhone, iPad,** and all devices with **Android, Windows Mobile, Nokia OS,** etc.

GET VIDEOS ON YOUR DEVICE

GET SHOPPING LIST

GET EXTRA CONTENTS FROM WEB SITE

QR CODE TIPS
If your device can not read QR Code:
- *The code is not sufficiently well lit*
- *You have not held your device still enough to read the code*
- *Dirt or other substances on the lens can cause an incorrect reading*
- *The surface on which the code is printed is dirty or damaged*
- *Your device can not read QR Codes*

HOW DO I USE THE QR CODE?
Start the program on your device, point the camera at the QR Code. What information does it contain?
- Ingredient list with quantities
- Extra content like recipe variations, tips, photos and video

List of QR code compatible software: http://tiramisuamoremio.com/qr-code-recipes-tiramisu/

The origin, the history of the most popular italian dessert

The origin, the history of the most popular Italian dessert, eaten worldwide:
the "tiramesù" (name in Venetian dialect)
by the pastry chef Roberto Linguanotto (called LOLY)
from: Italy - Veneto - Treviso

...."So, one day, I put together some simple and well-known ingredients and tried to make the whole "portionable": this is how this cake was born. It was immediately named "tiramesù" (pick-me-up)!
The ingredients, however simple, have to be first quality: from the coffee to the ladyfingers, from the mascarpone to the eggs.
I was persauded to have given birth to a successful cake, and this convinction was confirmed by the high quantity of portions served every day, and especially by the high number of customers that asked for a second serving!
The rest is history..., Tiramesù (afterwards renamed Tiramisù) is the best known Italian cake in the world, the most widely eaten and appreciated.
Now like then, at the Beccherie restaurant in Treviso, the Campeols make it this way, in its original round shape..."

Tiramesù has changed during the years – some ingredients have been replaced, some added.
In the mid 70s, in my ice-cream parlour "Glacia Shop" in Mestre (near Venice), I replaced the savoiardi (ladyfingers) with sponge cake, because -due to the high consumption of Tiramesù – I had to make it on large trays so that I could cut it into square slices.

Savoiardi may be replaced by:
- Sponge cake
- Pavesini cookies
- Pandoro cake (Christmas Tiramesù)
- Milk cookies
- Sardinia savoiardi (much bigger than the classic ones)

Mascarpone (all or half of it) may be replaced by:
- Ricotta cheese (Light Tiramesu')
- Custard
- Whipped cream
- Whipped egg whites

Egg yolks may be replaced by:
- Zabaglione

http://www.tiramesu.it

Original Recipe

INGREDIENTS

Makes 4-6 servings

- 1 Cup 8 Oz. (226 g.) Mascarpone Cheese room temperature)
- 6 Egg yolks
- 1 Cup 8 Oz. (226 g.) of Sugar
- 30 Ladyfingers
- 2 Cups Black Coffee (Espresso)
- Cocoa powder

DIRECTIONS

1. **Make** the coffee (espresso coffee); let cool in a bowl
2. **Whip** 6 egg yolks with sugar until stiff; fold the mascarpone cheese into yolk mixture thus obtaining a soft cream
3. **Dip** 15 Ladyfingers into the coffee, not to soak them
4. **Arrange** them in a line, in the middle of a round dish
5. **Spread** half of the cream over the Ladyfingers, then make another layer of Ladyfingers (soaked into coffee) and spread the remaining mascarpone cream over it
6. **Dust the** top the cocoa powder using a sifter
7. **Serve** chilled

Download Shopping list

Link additional content

www.tiramisuamoremio.com/tiramisu-original-recipe

Tiramisu Amore Mio

INGRE

DIENTS

Eggs

How to test if an egg is fresh:
One method to test the egg's freshness is by breaking the egg onto a flat plate.
The yolk of a very fresh egg will have a round and compact appearance and it will sit positioned quite high up in the middle of the egg. The white that surrounds it will be thick and stays close to the yolk. Over time, the egg white will become more transparent, as the carbon dioxide dissipates.
Very fresh eggs are ideal when preparing Tiramisù.

Mascarpone

Mascarpone originated in the area between Lodi and Abbiategrasso, Italy, southwest of Milan, probably in the late 16th or early 17th century. The name is said to come from mascarpa, a milk product made from the whey of stracchino (shortly aged cheese), or from mascarpia, the word in the local dialect for ricotta (although mascarpone is not made from whey, as ricotta is).
Mascarpone is milky-white in color and is easily sprinkle. It is used in various dishes of the Lombardy region of Italy, where it is a specialty. It is a main ingredient of modern Tiramisu. Mascarpone is recognized as Prodotto agroalimentare tradizionale (traditional regional food products).
The Mascarpone do not contain rennet and is suitable for vegetarians. It is made with full cream milk and citric acid (but no rennet): it is not cheese but dairy product.

Coffee

Espresso is a concentrated beverage brewed by forcing a small amount of nearly boiling water under pressure through finely ground coffee beans. Espresso often has a thicker consistency than coffee brewed by other methods, a higher concentration of suspended and dissolved solids, and crema (foam).

Ladyfingers And Sponge Cake

Ladyfingers are light and sweet sponge cakes roughly shaped like a large finger. They are called savoiardi in Italian (meaning "from Savoy"). Like other sponge cakes, ladyfingers traditionally contain no chemical leavening agent, and rely on air incorporated into the eggs for their "sponge" texture. They contain more flour than the average sponge cake. The mixture is piped through a pastry bag in short lines onto sheets, giving the cookies their notable shape.

Ricotta

Ricotta is an Italian dairy product made from sheep (or cow, goat, buffalo) milk whey left over from the production of cheese. Although typically referred to as ricotta cheese, ricotta is not properly a cheese because it is not produced by coagulation of casein. In fact, ricotta is safely eaten by individuals with casein intolerance.
Ricotta (literally meaning "recooked") uses the whey, a limpid, low-fat, nutritious liquid that is a by-product of cheese production.
Ricotta curds are creamy white in appearance, slightly sweet in taste, and contain around 13% fat. It is highly perishable. This use for the whey has ancient origins and is referred to by Cato the Elder.
While Italian ricotta is typically made from the whey of sheep, cow, goat, or water buffalo milk, the American product is almost always made of cow's milk whey. While both types are low in fat and sodium, the Italian version is naturally sweet, while the American is blander, slightly salty, and moister.

Spirits

AMARETTO - Usually a sweet liquor based on Almond. It has an amber colour and a typical almond scent.
FRANGELICO - Hazelnut liquor/cordial.
LIMONCELLO - It is obtained by the maceration of the rind of lemons in alcohol.
VIN SANTO: Vin Santo or Vino Santo (holy wine) is a style of Italian dessert wine. Traditional in Tuscany.
COINTREAU sources its bitter oranges from all over the world. It was originally called "Curaçao Blanco Triple Sec".
BAILEYS IRISH CREAM is an Irish whiskey and cream based liqueur, made by Gilbeys of Ireland rum is a distilled alcoholic beverage made from sugarcane by-products such as molasses, or directly from sugarcane juice, by a process of fermentation and distillation. The distillate, a clear liquid, is then usually aged in oak barrels.
RUM can be referred to by descriptors such as "ron viejo" ("old rum") and "ron añejo" ("aged rum").

Tools

Choose your tiramisu container. If you plan to just scoop out the tiramisu, there's no need to prepare the pan. Tip: A springform pan is a great tiramisu container.
However, if you plan to later invert the tiramisu from its pan onto a serving plate, first line the container (loaf pans, lasagna pan, bowl, individual dishes, etc.) with heavy plastic wrap, leaving some draped over the edges.

Our suggestions for prepare the Tiramisù (4-6 servings) you can use one of the following containers:

9x9 CAKE PAN (GLASS, PLASTIC, CERAMIC, ALUMINIUM)
DIFFERENT GLASSES (8 FL. OZ.):
BOWLS (8-12 FL.OZ)
CUPS

- 1 BOWL FOR BEAT THE YOLKS
- 1 BOWL FOR BEAT THE WHITES
- 1 CUP OR BOWLS FOR DIP THE COOKIES
- 1 WOODEN SPOON FOR FOLD THE EGGS WHITES
- 1 SPOON FOR THE CREAM
- 1 ELECTRIC MIXER (WHISK) OR FOOD PROCESSOR
- SIEVE FOR COCOA OR CANNELLA POWDER
- KNIFES (FOR CUT THE FRUITS OR DIFFERENT INGREDIENTS)
- CUTTING BOARD

FOR TIRAMISÙ WITH 2 DIFFERENT CREAMS:
1 EXTRA BOWL FOR DIVIDE THE CREAM

www.tiramisuamoremio.com/sponge-cake

Tiramisu Amore Mio

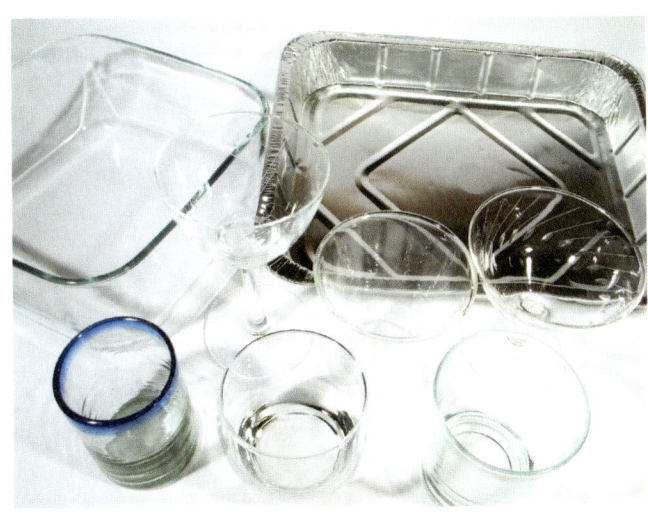
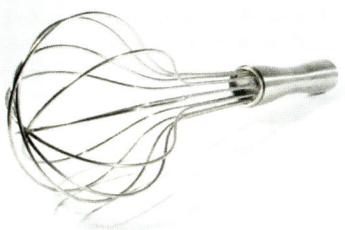

EXT
REC

RA
IPES

Sponge Cake

INGREDIENTS

MAKES **4-6** SERVINGS
- **3** EGGS
- **3,1 OZ.** (90 G.) FLOUR
- **3,1 OZ.** (90 G.) SUGAR
- **BUTTER** FOR GREASING THE CAKE PAN

DIRECTIONS

1. **Preheat** the oven to 356° F (180°)
2. **With** an electric mixer (or food processor), beat the eggs and sugar until stiff (about 12-15 minutes)
3. **Add** the flour with sieve stirring gently from the bottom to the top
4. **Greasing** with the butter the baking pan (10 Inch diameter - 26 cm) and dust with flour
5. **Add** the mixture to baking pan and then bake for 20 minutes

DOWNLOAD SHOPPING LIST

LINK ADDITIONAL CONTENT

www.tiramisuamoremio.com/sponge-cake

Ladyfinger

INGREDIENTS

Makes 4-6 servings
- 12 egg yolks
- 1 + 1/4 Cups 9.1 Oz. (260 g) sugar
- 8 egg whites
- 1 + 1/8 Cups 4.2 oz.(125 g) potato starch
- 1 + 1/8 Cups 4.2 oz. (25 g) flour
- Icing sugar

DIRECTIONS

1. **With** an electric mixer, beat the egg yolks with 1/4 of sugar (1/4 Cup) until the mixture has a consistency of mousse
2. **In** a separate bowl, beat the egg whites, until stiff, adding the rest of sugar
3. **Add** the potato starch with sieve stirring gently from the bottom to the top
4. **Combine** the whites with potato starch with the yolks mixture
5. **Add** the flour with sieve stirring gently from the bottom to the top
6. **Transfer** the mixture to pastry bag (with a plain 1/2 inch round tube) and pipe out onto prepared baking sheet with the nonstick oven paper
7. **With** a sieve add the Icing sugar
8. **Finally**, pass the cookies in a hot oven (356° F -180°) for 8-10 minutes

Download Shopping list

Link additional content

www.tiramisuamoremio.com/ladyfinger

How To Make Syrup Any type of Berries

INGREDIENTS

Ingredients for 20 Oz.
- 2.5 cups of fresh or frozen of berries
- 1 Tbsp Lemon juice - either fresh squeezed or bottled
- 2.5 cups Sugar
- 1 cup natural FROZEN CONCENTRATED FRUIT JUICE (grape, peach, apple or mixed)

Equipment
At least 1 large pot
Food processor
Colander
Cheesecloth

DIRECTIONS

1. **Wash** the berries in a colander of plain cold water
2. **Then** just drain off the water!
3. **Crush** the berries with food processor (for example hand mixer)
4. **Mix** the berries with the lemon juice and cook to a full boil Simmer until soft (5 to 10 minutes)
5. **Strain** the cooked berries through a colander
6. **Strain** again through cheesecloth
7. **Add** the sweetener
8. **Combine** the juice with 2.5 cups of sugar (or your other choice and quantity of sweetener) in a large saucepan, bring it to boiling, and simmer for 1 minute. Remove from heat and skim off any foam

Download Shopping list

Link additional content

www.tiramisuamoremio.com/any-barries-syrup

Orange syrup

INGREDIENTS

- **3 cups** fresh orange juice
- **9 Tbsp** sugar

Download Shopping list

DIRECTIONS

1. **Stir** all ingredients in heavy medium saucepan over medium heat until sugar dissolves
2. **Increase** heat and boil until syrup is reduced to 1 1/2 cups (about 20 minutes). Refrigerate until cold

www.tiramisuamoremio.com orange-syrup

Mint syrup

INGREDIENTS

- **1 cup** of mint leaves
- **2 cups** sugar
- **1 cup** water

Download Shopping list

DIRECTIONS

1. **Pick** 1 cup of mint leaves. Run them under water to clean them
2. **Add** to a saucepan along with 2 cups sugar and 1 cup water
3. **Bring** to a boil, and boil gently for a minute or two
4. **Stain** out the mint and let cool

www.tiramisuamoremio.com/mint-syrup

How To Make Basic Cream

INGREDIENTS

Makes 4-6 servings
- 1 Cup 8 Oz. (226 g.) Mascarpone Cheese (room temperature)
- 6 Egg yolks
- 1 Cup 8 Oz. (226 g.) of Sugar

DIRECTIONS

1. **Whip** 6 egg yolks with sugar until stiff ("egg yolk mixture")
2. **Fold** the mascarpone cheese into yolk mixture thus obtaining a soft cream

Download Shopping list

Link additional content

www.tiramisuamoremio.com/how-to-make-tiramisu-cream

How to Make Chocolate Cream

INGREDIENTS

Makes 4-6 servings
- Basic cream
- 2 or 3 Tbps cocoa powder

DIRECTIONS

1. **Divide** the "basic cream" in two parts (place the cream in two seprate bowls)
2. **In** one bowl add the Tbsp of cocoa powder (without sugar) in to the cream ("Chocolate cream")
3. **Gently** mix with a spoon

How to Make the Fruits Cream

INGREDIENTS

Makes 4-6 servings
1. Basic Cream
2. 4-6 Tbsp of Syrup

DIRECTIONS

Fruit cream with fresh fruits
1. **With any fruits: Blend** or purée mixture until well mixed thoroughly
2. **Add** the fruits mashed to the "egg yolk mixture" and stir ("Fruits cream")
3. **Add** the mascarpone cheese to the "Fruits cream"
4. **Beat** quickly at a reduced speed until creamy

www.tiramisuamoremio.com/how-to-make-chocolate-cream

TIRA

MISU

Tiramisù with Cinnamon and Coffee™

INGREDIENTS

Makes 4-6 servings

- 1 Cup 8 Oz. (226 g.) Mascarpone cheese (room temperature)
- 3 Eggs
- 4 Tbsp of sugar
- Pinch of salt
- 7 Oz. (200 g.) Sponge cake
- 1 Cup black coffee (room temperature)
- 2 Tbsp of cinnamon powder
- 2 Tbsp of cocoa powder

DIRECTIONS

HOW TO MAKE A BASIC CREAM

1. **With** an electric mixer, beat the egg whites until stiff. Add a pinch of salt and 1 Tbsp of sugar while mixing
2. **In** a separate bowl, beat the egg yolks, adding 3 Tbsp of sugar. Beat until the mixture has a consistency of mousse (about 3-4 minutes)
3. **Add** the mascarpone cheese to the egg yolk mixture. Beat quickly at a reduced speed until creamy. Using a wooden spoon, fold in the egg whites

HOW TO MAKE THE TIRAMISÙ

4. **In** a separate bowl combine coffee and a 1 Tbsp of cinnamon powder for dipping (room temperature)
5. **Cut** Sponge Cake into vertical slices exactly 1/4 inch thick. You can use the small pieces to fill in any gaps
6. **With** a pastry brush moisten the sponge cake with the coffee
7. **For** this dessert use one of the following containers: 9x9 cake pan (glass, plastic, ceramic, alluminium): Glasses (8 or more Fl. Oz.): Bowls (8-12 Fl. Oz.) place a layer of the "Basic cream" and then the sponge cake soaked in a coffee with cinnamon. Repeat for 2 layers.
8. **Sprinkle** the top with cinnamon powder and cocoa powder
9. **Chill** at least 2-3 hours before serving

Download Shopping list

Link additional content

www.tiramisuamoremio.com/tiramisu-cinnamon-coffee

Tiramisu Amore Mio

Double Chocolate Tiramisù™

INGREDIENTS

- Makes 4-6 servings
- 1 Cup 8 Oz. (226 g.) Mascarpone cheese (room temperature)
- 3 Eggs
- 4 Tbsp of sugar
- Pinch of salt
- 1 Tbsp of vanilla extract
- 3 Tbsp of water
- 5 Tbsp of cocoa powder
- 1/3 Cup 2.5 Oz. (60 g.) of grated white chocolate

Ladyfingers Quantity:
For Cake Pan (9x9) : 24 (12 for layers)
For Glasses and Bowls: 2-4 for glass (1-2 for layers)

Download Shopping list

DIRECTIONS

HOW TO MAKE THE BASIC CREAM

1. **With** an electric mixer, beat the egg whites until stiff. Add a pinch of salt and 1 Tbsp of sugar while mixing
2. **In** a separate bowl, beat the egg yolks, adding 3 Tbsp of sugar. Beat until the mixture has a consistency of mousse (about 3-4 minutes)
3. **Add** the mascarpone cheese to the egg yolk mixture. Beat quickly at a reduced speed until creamy. Using a wooden spoon, fold in the egg whites
4. **Divide** the basic cream in two parts for prepare two separtae cream (place the cream in two seprate bowls) (**Bowl n. 1 and Bowl n. 2**)

HOW TO MAKE THE WHITE CHOCOLATE CREAM (BOWL N. 1)

5. **In** bowl add 1/3 cup of white chocolate in to the cream ("White Chocolate cream")
6. **Gently** mix with a spoon

HOW TO MAKE THE DARK CHOCOLATE CREAM (BOWL N. 2)

7. **In** a bowl add 3 Tbsp of chocolate powder in to the cream ("Dark Chocolate cream")
8. **Gently** mix with a spoon

HOW TO MAKE THE TIRAMISÙ

9. **In** a separate bowl combine 1 Tbsp of vanilla extract and 3 Tbsp of water
10. **Dip** each Ladyfinger into the vanilla extract for only 2-3 seconds
11. **For** this dessert use one of the following containers: 9x9 cake pan (glass, plastic, ceramic, alluminium): Glasses (8 or more Fl. Oz.): Bowls (8-12 Fl. Oz.) place a layer of the "White Chocolate cream", then the Ladyfingers soaked in a vanilla and again place a layer of the "Dark Chocolate cream". Repeat for 2 layers.
12. **On** top add the cocoa powder
13. **Chill** at least 2-3 hours before serving

Link additional content

www.tiramisuamoremio.com/tiramisu-double-chocolate

Chocolate and Caramelized Orange Tiramisù™

INGREDIENTS

Makes 4-6 servings

- 1 Cup 8 Oz. (226 g.) mascarpone cheese (room temperature)
- 3 Eggs
- 10 Tbsp of sugar
- Pinch of salt
- 7 Oz. (200 g.) Sponge cake
- 1 Tbsp of vanilla extract
- 3 Tbsp of water
- 4 Tbsp of cocoa powder
- 2 Oranges (possibly organic)

Download Shopping list

DIRECTIONS

For caramelize the Oranges:

- Cut the Oranges in slices (0,3 inch. 1 cm)
- Melt 7 Tbps of sugar in a pot (low temperature)
- When you have the syrup, dip the slice of orange
- Put the slice of orange with caramel syrup on the paper (bake paper)
- Wait until it is cold

How to make the basic cream

1. **With** an electric mixer, beat the egg whites until stiff. Add a pinch of salt and 1 Tbsp of sugar while mixing
2. **In** a separate bowl, beat the egg yolks, adding 3 Tbsp of sugar. Beat until the mixture has a consistency of mousse (about 3-4 minutes)
3. **Add** the mascarpone cheese to the egg yolk mixture. Beat quickly at a reduced speed until creamy. Using a wooden spoon, fold in the egg whites
4. **Divide** the basic cream in two parts (place the cream in two seprate bowls) (**Bowl n. 1 and Bowl n. 2**)

How to make a chocolate cream (**Bowl n. 1**)

5. **In** a bowl add 4 Tbsp of cocoa powder in to the cream ("Chocolate cream")
6. **Gently** mix with a spoon

How to make the tiramisù

7. **In** a separate bowl combine a Tbsp of vanilla extract with 3 Tbsp of water
8. **Cut** Sponge Cake into vertical slices exactly 1/4 inch thick. You can use the small pieces to fill in any gaps
9. **With** a pastry brush moisten the sponge cake with the vanilla extract
10. **For** this dessert use one of the following containers: 9x9 cake pan (glass, plastic, ceramic, alluminium): Glasses (8 or more Fl. Oz.): Bowls (8-12 Fl. Oz.) place a layer of the "Chocolate cream", then the sponge cake soaked in a vanilla extract and slice of caramelized orange. Repeat for 2 layers.
11. **Chill** at least 2-3 hours before serving

Link additional content

www.tiramisuamoremio.com/tiramisu-chocolate-caramelize-orange

Tiramisù Cinnamon and Meringue™

INGREDIENTS

MAKES **4-6** SERVINGS
- 1/2 CUP **4 OZ.** (113 G.) MASCARPONE CHEESE (ROOM TEMPERATURE)
- 1/2 CUP **4 OZ.** (113 G.) RICOTTA CHEESE
- **3** EGGS
- **4** TBSP OF SUGAR
- PINCH OF SALT
- **1** CUP BLACK COFFEE (ROOM TEMPERATURE)
- **1** TBSP OF CINNAMON POWDER
- **2** CUPS OF MERINGUE
- **1** TBSP COCOA POWDER

LADYFINGERS Quantity:
For Cake Pan (9x9) : 24 (12 for layers)
For Glasses and Bowls: 2-4 for glass (1-2 for layers)

DIRECTIONS

HOW TO MAKE THE BASIC CREAM
1. **With** an electric mixer, beat the egg whites until stiff. Add a pinch of salt and 1 Tbsp of sugar while mixing
2. **In** a separate bowl, beat the egg yolks, adding 3 Tbsp of sugar. Beat until the mixture has a consistency of mousse (about 3-4 minutes)
3. **Add** the mascarpone and ricotta cheese to the egg yolk mixture. Beat quickly at a reduced speed until creamy. Using a wooden spoon, fold in the egg whites
4. **Divide** the basic cream in two parts (place the cream in two seprate bowls)

HOW TO MAKE THE CINNAMON CREAM
5. **In** one bowl add 1 Tbsp of cinnamon powder in to the cream ("Cinnamon cream")
6. **Gently** mix with a spoon

HOW TO MAKE THE TIRAMISÙ
7. **In** a separate bowl place the coffee for dipping (room temperature)
8. **Dip** each Ladyfinger into the coffee for only 2-3 seconds
9. **For** this dessert use one of the following containers: 9x9 cake pan (glass, plastic, ceramic, alluminium): Glasses (8 or more Fl. Oz.): Bowls (8-12 Fl. Oz.) place a layer of the "Cinnamon cream", then the Ladyfingers soaked in a coffee and 1 cup of meringues and again place a layer of the "Basic cream". Repeat for 2 layers.
10. **On** top add the meringues and cocoa powder
11. **Chill** at least 2-3 hours before serving

DOWNLOAD SHOPPING LIST

LINK ADDITIONAL CONTENT

www.tiramisuamoremio.com/tiramisu-cinnamon-meringues

Tiramisu Amore Mio

Tiramisù Chocolate and Pistachio™

INGREDIENTS

Makes 4-6 servings

- 1 Cup 8 Oz. (226 g.) mascarpone cheese (room temeprature)
- 3 eggs
- 4 Tbsp of sugar
- Pinch of salt
- 7 Oz. (200 g.) Sponge Cake
- 1 cup Almond milk
- 3 Tbsp of water
- 5 Tbsp of cocoa powder
- 4 Oz. (113 g.) of Pistachios without shell

Download Shopping list

DIRECTIONS

HOW TO MAKE THE BASIC CREAM

1. **With** an electric mixer, beat the egg whites until stiff. Add a pinch of salt and 1 Tbsp of sugar while mixing
2. **In** a separate bowl, beat the egg yolks, adding 3 Tbsp of sugar. Beat until the mixture has a consistency of mousse (about 3-4 minutes)
3. **Add** the mascarpone cheese to the egg yolk mixture. Beat quickly at a reduced speed until creamy. Using a wooden spoon, fold in the egg whites
4. **Divide** the basic cream in two parts (place the cream in two seprate bowls) (**Bowl n. 1 and Bowl n. 2**)

HOW TO MAKE THE PISTACHIO CREAM (**Bowl n. 1**)

5. **With** hand mixer reduce the pistachio in paste
6. **In** a bowl add the paste of pistachio in to the cream ("Pistachio cream")
7. **Mix** with a spoon (gently)

HOW TO MAKE A CHOCOLATE CREAM (**Bowl n. 2**)

8. **In** other bowl (with "Basic cream") add 4 Tbsp of cocoa powder ("Chocolate cream")
9. **Gently** mix with a spoon

HOW TO MAKE THE TIRAMISÙ

10. **In** a separate bowl combine 1 cup Almond milk and 3 Tbsp of water
11. **Cut** Sponge Cake into vertical slices exactly 1/4 inch thick. You can use the small pieces to fill in any gaps
12. **With** a pastry brush moisten the sponge cake with the almond milk
13. **For** this dessert use one of the following containers: 9x9 cake pan (glass, plastic, ceramic, alluminium): Glasses (8 or more Fl. Oz.): Bowls (8-12 Fl. Oz.) place a layer of the "Pistachio cream", then the sponge cake soaked in a almond milk, again place a layer of the "Chocolate cream". Repeat for 2 layers.
14. **Sprinkle** the top with 1 Tbsp of cocoa powder and some pistachios
15. **Chill** at least 2-3 hours before serving

Link additional content

www.tiramisuamoremio.com/tiramisu-chocolate-pistachio

Tiramisu Amore Mio

Tiramisù with Nougat and Cinnamon™

INGREDIENTS

Makes 4-6 servings

- 1/2 Cup 4 Oz. (113 g.) Mascarpone cheese (room temeprature)
- 1/2 Cup 4 Oz. (113 g.) Ricotta cheese
- 3 Eggs
- 4 Tbsp of sugar
- Pinch of salt
- 1 Cup black coffee (room temperature)
- 1 Tbsp of cinnamon powder
- 2-3 Tbsp of almonds
- 1 Cup of small pieces of nougat (Torrone)

Ladyfingers Quantity:
For Cake Pan (9x9) : 24 (12 for layers)
For Glasses and Bowls: 2-4 for glass (1-2 for layers)

Download Shopping list

DIRECTIONS

HOW TO MAKE THE BASIC CREAM

1. **With** an electric mixer, beat the egg whites until stiff. Add a pinch of salt and 1 Tbsp of sugar while mixing
2. **In** a separate bowl, beat the egg yolks, adding 3 Tbsp of sugar. Beat until the mixture has a consistency of mousse (about 3-4 minutes)
3. **Add** the mascarpone and ricotta cheese to the egg yolk mixture. Beat quickly at a reduced speed until creamy. Using a wooden spoon, fold in the egg whites

HOW TO MAKE THE TIRAMISÙ

4. **In** a separate bowl combine the coffee (room temperature) and 1 Tbsp of cinnamon powder
5. **Dip** each Ladyfinger into the coffee and cinnamon for only 2-3 seconds
6. **For** this dessert use one of the following containers: 9x9 cake pan (glass, plastic, ceramic, alluminium): Glasses (8 or more Fl. Oz.): Bowls (8-12 Fl. Oz.) place a layer of the "Basic cream", pieces of nougat (Torrone) and then the Ladyfingers soaked in a coffee with cinnamon. Repeat for 2 layers.
7. **On** top add the cinnamon powder, pieces of nougat (Torrone) and the almonds
8. **Chill** at least 2-3 hours before serving

Link additional content

www.tiramisuamoremio.com/tiramisu-nougat-cinnamon

Tiramisu Amore Mio

Chocolate and Granola Tiramisù™

INGREDIENTS

MAKES 4-6 SERVINGS
- 1/2 CUP 4 OZ. (113 G.) MASCARPONE CHEESE (ROOM TEMPERATURE)
- 1/2 CUP 4 OZ. (113 G.) RICOTTA CHEESE
- 3 EGGS
- 4 TBSP OF SUGAR
- PINCH OF SALT
- 1 CUP BLACK COFFEE (ROOM TEMPERATURE)
- 4 TBSP OF COCOA POWDER
- 2 CUPS OF GRANOLA

LADYFINGERS Quantity:
For Cake Pan (9x9) : 24 (12 for layers)
For Glasses and Bowls: 2-4 for glass (1-2 for layers)

DOWNLOAD SHOPPING LIST

DIRECTIONS

HOW TO MAKE THE BASIC CREAM
1. **With** an electric mixer, beat the egg whites until stiff. Add a pinch of salt and 1 Tbsp of sugar while mixing
2. **In** a separate bowl, beat the egg yolks, adding 3 Tbsp of sugar. Beat until the mixture has a consistency of mousse (about 3-4 minutes)
3. **Add** the mascarpone and ricotta cheese to the egg yolk mixture. Beat quickly at a reduced speed until creamy. Using a wooden spoon, fold in the egg whites
4. **Divide** the basic cream in two parts (place the cream in two seprate bowls) (**Bowl n. 1 and Bowl n. 2**)

HOW TO MAKE THE CHOCOLATE CREAM (BOWL N. 1)
5. **In** a bowl add 3 Tbsp of cocoa powder in to the "Basic cream" ("Chocolate cream")
6. **Gently** mix with a spoon

HOW TO MAKE THE GRANOLA CREAM (BOWL N. 2)
7. **In** other bowl (with "Basic cream") add the 2 cups of Granola ("Granola cream")
8. **Gently** mix with a spoon

HOW TO MAKE THE TIRAMISÙ
9. **In** a separate bowl place the coffee (room temperature)
10. **Dip** each Ladyfinger into the coffee for only 2-3 seconds
11. **Fo**r this dessert use one of the following containers: 9x9 cake pan (glass, plastic, ceramic, alluminium): Glasses (8 or more Fl. Oz.): Bowls (8-12 Fl. Oz.) place a layer of the "Chocolate cream" then the Ladyfingers soaked in a coffee and again place a layer of the "Granola cream". Repeat for 2 layers.
12. **On** top sprinkle the cocoa powder and granola
13. **Chill** at least 2-3 hours before serving

LINK ADDITIONAL CONTENT

www.tiramisuamoremio.com/tiramisu-chocolate-granola

Tiramisu Amore Mio

Cappuccino Tiramisù™

INGREDIENTS

Makes 4-6 servings

- 1/2 Cup 4 Oz. (113 g.) Mascarpone cheese (room temperature)
- 1/2 Cup 4 Oz. (113 g.) Ricotta cheese
- 3 Eggs
- 4 Tbsp of sugar
- Pinch of salt
- 1 Cup black coffee (room temperature)
- 1 Tbsp of cocoa powder
- 2 Tbsp of instant coffee
- 1 Cup of whipped cream

Ladyfingers Quantity:
For Cake Pan (9x9) : 24 (12 for layers)
For Glasses and Bowls: 2-4 for glass (1-2 for layers)

Download Shopping list

DIRECTIONS

how to make the basic cream

1. **With** an electric mixer, beat the egg whites until stiff. Add a pinch of salt and 1 Tbsp of sugar while mixing
2. **In** a separate bowl, beat the egg yolks, adding 3 Tbsp of sugar. Beat until the mixture has a consistency of mousse (about 3-4 minutes)

how to make the coffee cream

3. **Add** 2 Tbsp of instant Coffee, beat until the Coffee is well melted ("Coffee cream")
4. **Add** the mascarpone and ricotta cheese to the egg yolk mixture. Beat quickly at a reduced speed until creamy. Using a wooden spoon, fold in the egg whites

how to make the tiramisù

5. **In** a separate bowl place the coffee for dipping (room temperature)
6. **Dip** each Ladyfinger into the coffee or only 2-3 seconds
7. **For** this dessert use one of the following containers: 9x9 cake pan (glass, plastic, ceramic, alluminium): Glasses (8 or more Fl. Oz.): Bowls (8-12 Fl. Oz.) place a layer of the "Coffee cream" and then the Ladyfingers soaked in a coffee. Repeat for 2 layers.
8. **On** top add a whipped cream and cocoa powder
9. **Chill** at least 2-3 hours before serving

Link additional content

www.tiramisuamoremio.com/tiramisu-cappuccino

Tiramisu Amore Mio 43

Tiramisù Vanilla, Cinnamon and warm Chocolate™

INGREDIENTS

Makes 4-6 servings

- 1/2 Cup 4 Oz. (113 g.) mascarpone cheese (room temperature)
- 1/2 Cup 4 Oz. (113 g.) ricotta cheese
- 3 eggs
- 6 Tbsp of sugar
- Pinch of salt
- 7 Oz. (200 g.) Sponge Cake
- 1 cup black coffee (room temperature)
- 1 Tbsp vanilla exctract
- 3 Tbsp of cinnamon powder
- 2 Tbsp cocoa powder
- 1/2 cup of milk

Download Shopping list

DIRECTIONS

how to make the basic cream

1. **With** an electric mixer, beat the egg whites until stiff. Add a pinch of salt and 1 Tbsp of sugar while mixing
2. **In** a separate bowl, beat the egg yolks, adding 3 Tbsp of sugar. Beat until the mixture has a consistency of mousse (about 3-4 minutes)
3. **Add** the mascarpone cheese to the egg yolk mixture. Beat quickly at a reduced speed until creamy. Using a wooden spoon, fold in the egg whites
4. **Divide** the basic cream in two parts (place the cream in two seprate bowls) **(Bowl n. 1 and Bowl n. 2)**

how to make the cinnamon cream (Bowl n. 1)

5. **In** a bowl (with "Basic cream") add 2 Tbsp of cinnamon powder ("Cinnamon cream")
6. **Gently** mix with a spoon

how to make the vanilla cream (Bowl n. 2)

7. **In** other bowl (with "Basic cream") add the 1 Tbsp of vanilla exctract ("Vanilla cream")

how to make the tiramisù

8. **In** a separate bowl place a cup of black coffee for dipping (room temperature)
9. **Cut** Sponge Cake into vertical slices exactly 1/4 inch thick. You can use the small pieces to fill in any gaps
10. **With** a pastry brush moisten the sponge cake with the coffee
11. **Fo**r this dessert use one of the following containers: 9x9 cake pan (glass, plastic, ceramic, alluminium): Glasses (8 or more Fl. Oz.): Bowls (8-12 Fl. Oz.) place a layer of the "Cinnamon cream", then the sponge cake soaked in a coffee and again the layer of the "Vanilla cream". Repeat for 2 layers.
12. **Chill** at least 2-3 hours before serving

Warm Chocolate sauce (prepare before serving)
Melt 2 Tbsp of cocoa powder with 2 Tbsp of sugar and 1/2 cup of milk. Cook until dense
On top add cocoa powder and cinnamon powder

Link additional content

www.tiramisuamoremio.com/tiramisu-vanilla-cinnamon-warm-chocolate

Tiramisu Amore Mio

Chocolate and Mint Tiramisù™

INGREDIENTS

Makes 4-6 servings

- 1 Cup 8 Oz. (226 g.) Mascarpone cheese (room temperature)
- 3 Eggs
- 4 Tbsp of sugar
- Pinch of salt
- 4 Tbsp of mint syrup
- 3 Tbsp of water
- 4 Tbsp of cocoa powder
- 1 Cup Red currant decoration

Ladyfingers Quantity:
For Cake Pan (9x9) : 24 (12 for layers)
For Glasses and Bowls: 2-4 for glass (1-2 for layers)

Download Shopping list

DIRECTIONS

HOW TO MAKE THE BASIC CREAM

1. **With** an electric mixer, beat the egg whites until stiff. Add a pinch of salt and 1 Tbsp of sugar while mixing
2. **In** a separate bowl, beat the egg yolks, adding 3 Tbsp of sugar. Beat until the mixture has a consistency of mousse (about 3-4 minutes)
3. **Add** the mascarpone cheese to the egg yolk mixture. Beat quickly at a reduced speed until creamy. Using a wooden spoon, fold in the egg whites
4. **Divide** the basic cream in two parts (place the cream in two seprate bowls) (**Bowl n. 1** and **Bowl n. 2**)

HOW TO MAKE THE MINT CREAM (Bowl n. 1)

5. **In** a bowl add 2 Tbsp of mint syrup in to the cream ("Mint cream")
6. **Gently** mix with a spoon

HOW TO MAKE THE CHOCOLATE CREAM (Bowl n. 2)

7. **In** the other bowl add 4 Tbsp of cocoa powder in to the cream ("Chocolate cream")
8. **Gently** mix with a spoon

HOW TO MAKE THE TIRAMISÙ

9. **In** a separate bowl combine 1 Tbsp of mint syrup and 3 Tbsp of water
10. **Dip** each Ladyfinger into the mint for only 2-3 seconds
11. **For** this dessert use one of the following containers: 9x9 cake pan (glass, plastic, ceramic, alluminium): Glasses (8 or more Fl. Oz.): Bowls (8-12 Fl. Oz.) place a layer of the "Chocolate cream," and then the Ladyfingers soaked in mint syrup and again place a layer of the "Mint cream". Repeat for 2 layers.
12. **Add** on top the fresh red currant
13. **Chill** at least 2-3 hours before serving

Link additional content

www.tiramisuamoremio.com/tiramisu-chocolate-mint

Tiramisu Amore Mio

Tiramisù with Crunchy Caramel™

INGREDIENTS

Makes 4-6 servings

- 1 Cup 8 Oz. (226 g.) Mascarpone Cheese (room temperature)
- 3 Eggs
- 4 Tbsp Of Sugar
- Pinch Of Salt
- 12 Ladyfingers For Decorations (Optional)
- 7 Oz. Sponge Cake (200 g.)
- 1 Cup Black Coffee for dipping (room temperature)

For Caramel

- 10 Oz. (300 g.) Caster Sugar

Download Shopping list

DIRECTIONS

Prepare the caramel

Cook sugar until it's completely melted. Use a nonstick pan on low/medium fire. Pay attention, stir and when the color is golden/brown the caramel is done.

On the nonstick oven paper or on flexible silicon mat with nonstick surface, when the caramel is cool enough to form a fine thread, hold with a pastry brush (silicon) and dip them into the caramel. Using a quick flicking motion drizzle the caramel.

How to make the basic cream

1. **With** an electric mixer, beat the egg whites until stiff. Add a pinch of salt and 1 Tbsp of sugar while mixing
2. **In** a separate bowl, beat the egg yolks, adding 3 Tbsp of sugar. Beat until the mixture has a consistency of mousse (about 3-4 minutes)
3. **Add** the mascarpone cheese to the egg yolk mixture. Beat quickly at a reduced speed until creamy. Using a wooden spoon, fold in the egg whites

How to make the tiramisù

4. **In** a separate bowl place a cup of black coffee for dipping (room temperature)
5. **Cut** Sponge Cake into vertical slices exactly 1/4 inch thick. You can use the small pieces to fill in any gaps
6. **With** a pastry brush moisten the sponge cake with the coffee
7. **In** a container (in plastic, glass or alluminium. Size 9x9) or individual water glasses (about 8 fluid Oz.), place a layer of the cream, crunchy caramel and then the sponge cake soaked in a coffee. Repeat for 2 layers.
8. **Optional**: Serve on the plate and decorate with Ladyfingers
9. **Chill** at least 2-3 hours before serving

Link additional content

www.tiramisuamoremio.com/tiramisu-crunchy-caramel

Tiramisu Amore Mio

TIRA

Recipes

MISU

with

Alcohol

Tiramisù Chocolate, Cherries and Rum™

INGREDIENTS

Makes 4-6 servings

- 1/2 Cup 4 Oz. (113 g.) Mascarpone cheese (room temperature)
- 1/2 Cup 4 Oz. (113 g.) Ricotta cheese
- 3 Eggs
- 4 Tbsp of sugar
- Pinch of salt
- 4 Tbsp cocoa powder
- 1/2 cups Dark chocolate (break a tablet in small pieces)
- 7 Oz. (200 g.) Sponge cake
- 1 Cup of rum
- 2 Tbsp per person of cherry marmelade or cherries in syrup

Download Shopping list

DIRECTIONS

HOW TO MAKE THE BASIC CREAM

1. **With** an electric mixer, beat the egg whites until stiff. Add a pinch of salt and 1 Tbsp of sugar while mixing.
2. **In** a separate bowl, beat the egg yolks, adding 3 Tbsp of sugar. Beat until the mixture has a consistency of mousse (about 3-4 minutes)
3. **Add** the mascarpone cheese to the egg yolk mixture. Beat quickly at a reduced speed until creamy. Using a wooden spoon, fold in the egg whites

HOW TO MAKE THE CHOCOLATE CREAM

4. **Add** 4 Tbsp of cocoa powder in the basic cream ("Chocolate cream")
5. **Gently** mix with a spoon)

HOW TO MAKE THE TIRAMISÙ

6. **In** a separate bowl place the Rum for dipping
7. **Cut** Sponge Cake into vertical slices exactly 1/4 inch thick. You can use the small pieces to fill in any gaps
8. **With** a pastry brush moisten the sponge cake with the Rum
9. **For** this dessert use one of the following containers: 9x9 cake pan (glass, plastic, ceramic, alluminium): Glasses (8 or more Fl. Oz.): Bowls (8-12 Fl. Oz.) place a layer of the "Chocolate cream", cherries marmelade (or cherries in syrup) and pieces of dark chocolate and then the sponge cake soaked in a Rum. Repeat for 2 layers.
10. **Add** on top the Cherries in Syrup
11. **Chill** at least 2-3 hours before serving

Link additional content

www.tiramisuamoremio.com/tiramisu-chocolate-cherry-rum

Tiramisu Amore Mio

Irish Coffee Tiramisù™

INGREDIENTS

Makes 4-6 servings
- 1 Cup 8 Oz. (226 g.) Mascarpone cheese (room temperature)
- 3 Eggs
- 4 Tbsp of sugar
- Pinch of salt
- 7 Oz. (200 g.) Sponge cake
- 1-2 Cups of irish whisky
- 3 Tbsp of instant coffee
- 1 Cup 8 Oz. (226 g.) whipped heavy cream

Download Shopping list

DIRECTIONS

HOW TO MAKE THE BASIC CREAM

1. **With** an electric mixer, beat the egg whites until stiff. Add a pinch of salt and 1 Tbsp of sugar while mixing
2. **In** a separate bowl, beat the egg yolks, adding 3 Tbsp of sugar. Beat until the mixture has a consistency of mousse (about 3-4 minutes)

HOW TO MAKE THE COFFEE CREAM

3. **Add** 2 Tbsp of instant Coffee until is melt ("Coffee cream")
4. **Gently** mix with a spoon
5. **Add** the mascarpone cheese to the egg yolk mixture. Beat quickly at a reduced speed until creamy. Using a wooden spoon, fold in the egg whites

HOW TO MAKE THE TIRAMISÙ

6. **In** a separate bowl place the cups of Irish Whisky for dipping
7. **Cut** Sponge Cake into vertical slices exactly 1/4 inch thick. You can use the small pieces to fill in any gaps
8. **With** a pastry brush moisten the sponge cake with the Whisky
9. **With** an electric mixer, beat the "heavy cream" until has a soft consistency (similar the foam of cappuccino)
10. **For** this dessert use one of the following containers: 9x9 cake pan (glass, plastic, ceramic, alluminium): Glasses (8 or more Fl. Oz.): Bowls (8-12 Fl. Oz.) place a layer of the "Coffee cream" and then the sponge cake soaked in a Whisky. Repeat for 2 layers.
11. **Add** on top the whipped cream
12. **Chill** at least 2-3 hours before serving

Link additional content

www.tiramisuamoremio.com/tiramisu-irish-coffee

Tiramisu Amore Mio

Whisky Cream Tiramisù™

INGREDIENTS

Makes 4-6 servings

- 1 Cup 8 Oz. (226 g.) Mascarpone cheese (room temperature)
- 4 Eggs
- 5 Tbsp of sugar
- Pinch of salt
- 7 Oz. (200 g.) Sponge cake
- 1-2 Cups of whisky
- 2 Cups of baileys (or any whisky cream liquor)
- 4 Tbsp cocoa powder
- 1/2 cups Dark chocolate (broken a tablet in small pieces)

Download Shopping list

DIRECTIONS

How to make the Baileys cream

1. **With** an electric mixer, beat the egg whites until stiff. Add a pinch of salt and 1 Tbsp of sugar while mixing.
2. **In** a separate bowl, beat the egg yolks, adding 4 Tbsp of sugar. Beat until the mixture has a consistency of mousse (about 3-4 minutes)
3. **Add** the cup of Baileys until is melt ("Baileys cream")
4. **Gently** mix with a spoon
5. **Add** the mascarpone cheese to the egg yolk mixture. Beat quickly at a reduced speed until creamy. Using a wooden spoon, fold in the egg whites.

How to make the Tiramisù

6. **In** a separate bowl place the cups of the Whisky for dipping
7. **Cut** Sponge Cake into vertical slices exactly 1/4 inch thick. You can use the small pieces to fill in any gaps
8. **With** a pastry brush moisten the sponge cake with the Whisky
9. **For** this dessert use one of the following containers: 9x9 cake pan (glass, plastic, ceramic, alluminium): Glasses (8 or more Fl. Oz.): Bowls (8-12 Fl. Oz.) place a layer of the "Baileys cream", pieces of dark chocolate and then the sponge cake soaked in a Whisky. Repeat for 2 layers.
10. **Sprinkle** the top with cocoa powder
11. **Chill** at least 2-3 hours before serving

Link additional content

www.tiramisuamoremio.com/tiramisu-baileys-whisky

Tiramisu Amore Mio

Tiramisù Chocolate, Coffee and Rum™

INGREDIENTS

Makes 4-6 servings

- 1 Cup 8 Oz. (226 g.) Mascarpone cheese (room temperature)
- 3 Eggs
- 4 Tbsp of sugar
- Pinch of salt
- 7 Oz. (200 g.) Sponge cake
- 1 Cup black coffee (room temperature)
- 1/2 cups of Rum
- 2 Tbsp of instant coffee
- 5 Tbsp of cocoa powder
- 1 cup coffee beans or chocolate chips

Download Shopping list

DIRECTIONS

HOW TO MAKE THE BASIC CREAM

1. **With** an electric mixer, beat the egg whites until stiff. Add a pinch of salt and 1 Tbsp of sugar while mixing
2. **In** a separate bowl, beat the egg yolks, adding 3 Tbsp of sugar. Beat until the mixture has a consistency of mousse (about 3-4 minutes)
3. **Add** the mascarpone cheese to the egg yolk mixture. Beat quickly at a reduced speed until creamy. Using a wooden spoon, fold in the egg whites
4. **Divide** the "Basic cream" in two parts (place the cream in two seprate bowls) **(Bowl n. 1 and Bowl n. 2)**

HOW TO MAKE THE COFFEE CREAM (Bowl n. 1)

5. **In** one of the two bowls, add 2 Tbsp of instant coffee ("Coffee cream")
6. **Gently** mix with a spoon

HOW TO MAKE THE CHOCOLATE CREAM (Bowl n. 2)

7. **In** other bowl (with "Basic cream") add the 4 Tbsp of cocoa powder ("Chocolate cream")

HOW TO MAKE THE TIRAMISÙ

8. **In** a separate bowl combine the coffee and Rum (room temperature)
9. **Cut** Sponge Cake into vertical slices exactly 1/4 inch thick. You can use the small pieces to fill in any gaps
10. **With** a pastry brush moisten the sponge cake with the coffee and Rum
11. **For** this dessert use one of the following containers: 9x9 cake pan (glass, plastic, ceramic, alluminium): Glasses (8 or more Fl. Oz.): Bowls (8-12 Fl. Oz.) place a layer of the "Chocolate cream", then the sponge cake soaked in a mixture of coffee and Rum and again place a layer of the "Coffee cream". Repeat for 2 layers.
12. **Sprinkle** the top with cocoa powder and some coffee beans or chocolate chips
13. **Chill** at least 2-3 hours before serving

Link additional content

www.tiramisuamoremio.com/tiramisu-chocolate-coffee-rum

Tiramisu Amore Mio

Tiramisù Toffee cream, Pear and Amaretto™

INGREDIENTS

MAKES 4-6 SERVINGS

- 1 Cup 8 Oz. (226 g.) Mascarpone cheese (room temperature)
- 3 Eggs
- 11 Tbsp of sugar
- Pinch of salt
- 1 Cup black coffee (room temperature)
- 1 cup of Ameretto liquor
- 1/2 cups toffee cream
- 1 Pear in thin slices (caramelized)
- 1 Cup of ameretti cookies

LADYFINGERS Quantity:
For Cake Pan (9x9) : 24 (12 for layers)
For Glasses and Bowls: 2-4 for glass (1-2 for layers)

DOWNLOAD SHOPPING LIST

DIRECTIONS

FOR CARAMELIZE THE PEAR:
- Cut the pear in slices (1/4 inch. 0,5 cm)
- Melt 7 spoons of sugar in a pot (low temperature)
- When you'll have the syrup, dip the slice of pear
- Put the slice of pear with caramel syrup on the paper (bake paper)
- Wait until is cold

HOW TO MAKE THE BASIC CREAM

1. **With** an electric mixer, beat the egg whites until stiff. Add a pinch of salt and 1 Tbsp of sugar while mixing
2. **In** a separate bowl, beat the egg yolks, adding 3 Tbsp of sugar. Beat until the mixture has a consistency of mousse (about 3-4 minutes)
3. **Add** the mascarpone cheese to the egg yolk mixture. Beat quickly at a reduced speed until creamy. Using a wooden spoon, fold in the egg whites

HOW TO MAKE THE TIRAMISÙ

4. **In** a separate bowl combine the coffee (room temperature) and Amaretto for dipping
5. **Dip** each Ladyfinger into the coffee and Amaretto for only 2-3 seconds
6. **For** this dessert use one of the following containers: 9x9 cake pan (glass, plastic, ceramic, alluminium): Glasses (8 or more Fl. Oz.): Bowls (8-12 Fl. Oz.) place a layer of the "Basic cream," the slice of caramelized pear, toffee cream and and Amaretti cookies, then the Ladyfingers soaked in a mixture of coffee and Amaretto. Repeat for 2 layers.
7. **Chill** at least 2-3 hours before serving

LINK ADDITIONAL CONTENT

www.tiramisuamoremio.com/tiramisu-toffee-cream-pear-amaretto

Tiramisu Amore Mio

TIRA

Recipes

MISU

with

Fruits

Banana Tiramisù™

INGREDIENTS

Makes 4-6 servings

- 1 Cup 8 Oz. (226 g.) Mascarpone cheese (room temperature)
- 3 Eggs
- 4 Tbsp of sugar
- Pinch of salt
- 4 peeled bananas
- 1 Tbsp of cocoa powder
- 1 Tbsp of vanilla extract
- 3 Tbsp of water
- Half lemon

Ladyfingers Quantity:
For Cake Pan (9x9) : 24 (12 for layers)
For Glasses and Bowls: 2-4 for glass (1-2 for layers)

Download Shopping list

DIRECTIONS

HOW TO MAKE THE BASIC CREAM

1. **With** an electric mixer, beat the egg whites until stiff. Add a pinch of salt and 1 Tbsp of sugar while mixing
2. **In** a separate bowl, beat the egg yolks, adding 3 Tbsp of sugar. Beat until the mixture has a consistency of mousse (about 3-4 minutes)

HOW TO MAKE THE BANANA CREAM

3. **Slice** 3 bananas into small chunks or pieces
4. **Place** the pieces into a food processor or blender
5. **Blend** or purée mixture until well mixed thoroughly
6. **Add** one teaspoon of lemon juice to prevent browning
7. **Add** the banana mashed to the egg yolk mixture stir ("Banana cream")
8. **Add** the mascarpone cheese to the "Banana cream". Beat quickly at a reduced speed until creamy. Using a wooden spoon, fold in the egg whites
9. **Cut** the banana (remain) in thin slice add some drops with lemon juice to prevent browning

HOW TO MAKE THE TIRAMISÙ

10. **In** a separate bowl combine the vanilla extract and 3 Tbsp of water
11. **Dip** each Ladyfinger into the vanilla extract for only 2-3 seconds
12. **For** this dessert use one of the following containers: 9x9 cake pan (glass, plastic, ceramic, alluminium): Glasses (8 or more Fl. Oz.): Bowls (8-12 Fl. Oz.) place a layer of the "Banana cream" some slice of banana and then the Ladyfingers soaked in a vanilla extract. Repeat for 2 layers.
13. **Add** on the top the cocoa powder
14. **Chill** at least 2-3 hours before serving

Link additional content

www.tiramisuamoremio.com/tiramisu-banana

Tiramisu Amore Mio

Raspberries and Honey Tiramisù™

INGREDIENTS

Makes 4-6 servings

- 1/2 Cup 4 Oz. (113 g.) Mascarpone cheese (room temperature)
- 1/2 Cup 4 Oz. (113 g.) Ricotta cheese
- 3 Eggs
- 4 Tbsp of sugar
- Pinch of salt
- 7 Oz. (200 g.) Sponge cake
- 1 Cup almond milk
- 3 Tbsp of water
- 1 Tbsp lemon juice
- 3 Tbsp of honey
- 25 Oz. (700 g.) of fresh Raspberries

Download Shopping list

DIRECTIONS

Prepare the Honey and Rasperry sauce

Gently wash the fresh raspberries, take a container, pour (**12 Oz.**. Half of total that we have) the raspberries into it and crush them. Add lemon juice and honey into the container and mix well. Combine the mixture with raspberries and blend with hand mixer. Sift out the mixture (to eliminate the seeds)

how to make the basic cream

1. **With** an electric mixer, beat the egg whites until stiff. Add a pinch of salt and 1 Tbsp of sugar while mixing
2. **In** a separate bowl, beat the egg yolks, adding 3 Tbsp of sugar. Beat until the mixture has a consistency of mousse (about 3-4 minutes)
3. **Add** the mascarpone cheese and ricotta cheese to the egg yolk mixture. Beat quickly at a reduced speed until creamy. Using a wooden spoon, fold in the egg whites
4. **Divide** the basic cream in two parts (place the cream in two seprate bowls)

how to make the honey and raspberry cream

5. **In** one bowl add 2 Tbsp of "Honey and Rasperry sauce" in to the cream ("Honey and Rasperry cream")
6. **Gently** mix with a spoon

how to make the tiramisù

7. **In** a separate bowl combine 1 cup Almond milk and 3 Tbsp of water
8. **Cut** Sponge Cake into vertical slices exactly 1/4 inch thick. You can use the small pieces to fill in any gaps
9. **With** a pastry brush moisten the sponge cake with the Almond milk
10. **For** this dessert use one of the following containers: 9x9 cake pan (glass, plastic, ceramic, alluminium): Glasses (8 or more Fl. Oz.): Bowls (8-12 Fl. Oz.) place a layer of the "Honey and Rasperry cream" and then the sponge cake soaked in Almound milk and again place the layer with "Basic cream". Repeat for 2 layers.
11. **Add** the raspberries on the top.(**12 Oz.**)
12. **Chill** at least 2-3 hours before serving

Link additional content

www.tiramisuamoremio.com/tiramisu-raspberry-honey

Tiramisu Amore Mio

Tiramisù with "Mixed barries"™

INGREDIENTS

MAKES 4-6 SERVINGS
- 1 Cup 8 Oz. (226 g.) Mascarpone cheese (room temperature)
- 3 Eggs
- 4 Tbsp of sugar
- Pinch of salt
- 12 Ladyfingers for decorations (optional)
- 7 Oz. (200 g.) Sponge cake.
- 1 Cup blueberry syrup
- 3 Tbsp water
- 2 Cups with mixed barries

Download Shopping list

DIRECTIONS

HOW TO MAKE THE BASIC CREAM

1. **With** an electric mixer, beat the egg whites until stiff. Add a pinch of salt and 1 Tbsp of sugar while mixing
2. **In** a separate bowl, beat the egg yolks, adding 3 Tbsp of sugar. Beat until the mixture has a consistency of mousse (about 3-4 minutes)
3. **Add** the mascarpone cheese to the egg yolk mixture. Beat quickly at a reduced speed until creamy. Using a wooden spoon, fold in the egg whites

HOW TO MAKE THE TIRAMISÙ

4. **In** a separate bowl combine a cup of blueberry syrup and 3 Tbsp of water for dipping
5. **Cut** Sponge Cake into vertical slices exactly 1/4 inch thick. You can use the small pieces to fill in any gaps
6. **With** a pastry brush moisten the sponge cake with the blueberry syrup
7. **Fo**r this dessert use one of the following containers: 9x9 cake pan (glass, plastic, ceramic, alluminium): Glasses (8 or more Fl. Oz.): Bowls (8-12 Fl. Oz.) place a layer of the "Basic cream", and then the sponge cake soaked in a blueberry syrup. Repeat for 2 layers.
8. **Optional**: Serve on the plate and decorate with Ladyfingers and forest fruits
9. **Chill** at least 2-3 hours before serving

Link additional content

www.tiramisuamoremio.com/tiramisu-forest-fruits

Tiramisu Amore Mio

Tiramisù with Fresh Strawberries™

INGREDIENTS

MAKES 4-6 SERVINGS
- 1/2 Cup 4 Oz. (113 g.) Mascarpone cheese (room temperature)
- 1/2 Cup 4 Oz. (113 g.) Ricotta cheese
- 3 Eggs
- 4 Tbsp of sugar
- Pinch of salt
- 3 Tbsp of water
- 1 Cup strawberry syrup
- 10 Strawberries cut into 1/4-1/2 inch thick slices

LADYFINGERS Quantity:
For Cake Pan (9x9) : 24 (12 for layers)
For Glasses and Bowls: 2-4 for glass (1-2 for layers)

DOWNLOAD SHOPPING LIST

DIRECTIONS

HOW TO MAKE THE BASIC CREAM
1. **With** an electric mixer, beat the egg whites until stiff. Add a pinch of salt and 1 Tbsp of sugar while mixing
2. **In** a separate bowl, beat the egg yolks, adding 3 Tbsp of sugar. Beat until the mixture has a consistency of mousse (about 3-4 minutes)
3. **Add** the mascarpone and ricotta cheeses to the egg yolk mixture. Beat quickly at a reduced speed until creamy. Using a wooden spoon, fold in the egg whites

HOW TO MAKE THE TIRAMISÙ
4. **In** a separate bowl combine 1 cup strawberry syrup and 3 Tbsp of water
5. **Dip** each Ladyfinger into the strawberry syrup for only 2-3 seconds
6. **For** this dessert use one of the following containers: 9x9 cake pan (glass, plastic, ceramic, alluminium): Glasses (8 or more Fl. Oz.): Bowls (8-12 Fl. Oz.) place a layer of the "Basic cream" and then the Ladyfingers soaked in a strawberry syrup. Repeat for 2 layers.
7. **On** top add the fresh strawberries
8. **Chill** at least 2-3 hours before serving

LINK ADDITIONAL CONTENT

www.tiramisuamoremio.com/tiramisu-fresh-strawberries

Tiramisu Amore Mio

Tiramisù with Fresh Cherries™

INGREDIENTS

MAKES 4-6 SERVINGS

- 1/2 Cup 4 Oz. (113 g.) Mascarpone cheese (room temperature)
- 1/2 Cup 4 Oz. (113 g.) Ricotta cheese
- 3 Eggs
- 4 Tbsp of sugar
- Pinch of salt
- 1 Cup of cherry syrup
- 3 Tbsp water
- 4-6 Fresh Cherries per person

Ladyfingers Quantity:
For Cake Pan (9x9) : 24 (12 for layers)
For Glasses and Bowls: 2-4 for glass (1-2 for layers)

DIRECTIONS

HOW TO MAKE THE BASIC CREAM

1. **With** an electric mixer, beat the egg whites until stiff. Add a pinch of salt and 1 Tbsp of sugar while mixing
2. **In** a separate bowl, beat the egg yolks, adding 3 Tbsp of sugar. Beat until the mixture has a consistency of mousse (about 3-4 minutes)
3. **Add** the mascarpone and ricotta cheese to the egg yolk mixture. Beat quickly at a reduced speed until creamy. Using a wooden spoon, fold in the egg whites
4. **Divide** the basic cream in two parts (place the cream in two seprate bowls)

HOW TO MAKE THE CHERRY CREAM

5. **In** one bowl (with "Basic cream") add 2 Tbsp of cherry syrup ("Cherry cream")
6. **Gently** mix with a spoon

HOW TO MAKE THE TIRAMISÙ

7. **In** a separate bowl combine 1 cup cherry syrup and 3 Tbsp of water
8. **Dip** each Ladyfinger into the cherry syrup for only 2-3 seconds
9. **For** this dessert use one of the following containers: 9x9 cake pan (glass, plastic, ceramic, alluminium): Glasses (8 or more Fl. Oz.): Bowls (8-12 Fl. Oz.) place a layer of the "Cherries cream", then the Ladyfingers soaked in a cherry syrup and place a layer of the "Basic cream". Repeat for 2 layers.
10. **On the** top place the fresh cherries
11. **Chill** at least 2-3 hours before serving

Download Shopping list

Link additional content

www.tiramisuamoremio.com/tiramisu-fresh-cherry

Tiramisu Amore Mio

Tiramisù with Fresh Orange and Chocolate™

INGREDIENTS

Makes 4-6 servings

- 1 Cup 8 Oz. (226 g.) Mascarpone cheese (room temperature)
- 3 Eggs
- 4 Tbsp of sugar
- Pinch of salt
- 3 Tbsp of orange syrup (for dip)
- 3 Tbsp of water
- 2 Tbsp of orange syrup (for the cream)
- 7 Oz. (200 g.) Sponge cake
- 4 Tbsp of chocolate chips
- 1 Fresh orange cut in thin slices (possibly organic)

Download Shopping list

DIRECTIONS

HOW TO MAKE THE BASIC CREAM

1. **With** an electric mixer, beat the egg whites until stiff. Add a pinch of salt and 1 Tbsp of sugar while mixing
2. **In** a separate bowl, beat the egg yolks, adding 3 Tbsp of sugar. Beat until the mixture has a consistency of mousse (about 3-4 minutes)
3. **Add** the mascarpone cheese to the egg yolk mixture. Beat quickly at a reduced speed until creamy. Using a wooden spoon, fold in the egg whites

HOW TO MAKE THE ORANGE CREAM

4. **Divide** the basic cream in two parts (place the cream in two seprate bowls)
5. **In** one bowl add 2 Tbsp of organge syrup in to the cream ("Orange cream")
6. **Gently** mix with a spoon

HOW TO MAKE THE TIRAMISÙ

7. **In** a separate bowl combine 3 Tbsp of Orange syrup and 3 Tbsp of water
8. **Cut** Sponge Cake into vertical slices exactly 1/4 inch thick. You can use the small pieces to fill in any gaps
9. **With** a pastry brush moisten the sponge cake with the orange syrup
10. **Fo**r this dessert use one of the following containers: 9x9 cake pan (glass, plastic, ceramic, alluminium): Glasses (8 or more Fl. Oz.): Bowls (8-12 Fl. Oz.) place a layer of the "Orange cream", then the sponge cake soaked in a orange syrup and some chocolate chips and again place the layer with "Basic cream". Repeat for 2 layers.
11. **Decorated** with the slice of fresh orange and chocolate chips
12. **Chill** at least 2-3 hours before serving

Link additional content

www.tiramisuamoremio.com/tiramisu-fresh-orange-chocolate

Tiramisu Amore Mio

Tiramisù with Blueberries and Wafers™

INGREDIENTS

MAKES 4-6 SERVINGS

- 1/2 Cup 4 Oz. (113 G.) Mascarpone cheese (room temperature)
- 1/2 Cup 4 Oz. (113 G.) Ricotta cheese
- 3 Eggs
- 4 Tbsp of sugar
- Pinch of salt
- 2 wafers per person
- 2 Cups of fresh blueberries
- 1 Cup blueberry syrup
- 3 Tbsp of water

Ladyfingers Quantity:
For Cake Pan (9x9) : 24 (12 for layers)
For Glasses and Bowls: 2-4 for glass (1-2 for layers)

DIRECTIONS

HOW TO MAKE THE BASIC CREAM

1. **With** an electric mixer, beat the egg whites until stiff. Add a pinch of salt and 1 Tbsp of sugar while mixing
2. **In** a separate bowl, beat the egg yolks, adding 3 Tbsp of sugar. Beat until the mixture has a consistency of mousse (about 3-4 minutes)
3. **Add** the mascarpone cheese and ricotta cheese to the egg yolk mixture. Beat quickly at a reduced speed until creamy. Using a wooden spoon, fold in the egg whites

HOW TO MAKE THE TIRAMISÙ

4. **In** a separate bowl combine 1 cup blueberry syrup and 3 Tbsp of water
5. **Dip** each Ladyfinger into the blueberry syrup for only 2-3 seconds
6. **For** this dessert use one of the following containers: 9x9 cake pan (glass, plastic, ceramic, alluminium): Glasses (8 or more Fl. Oz.): Bowls (8-12 Fl. Oz.) place a layer of the "Basic cream" and then the Ladyfingers soaked in a blueberry syrup some fresh bleberries and wafer cookies. Repeat for 2 layers.
7. **Add** on top fresh blueberries
8. **Chill** at least 2-3 hours before serving

Download Shopping list

Link additional content

www.tiramisuamoremio.com/tiramisu-blueberry-wafer

Tiramisu Amore Mio

Tiramisù Vanilla, Chocolate and Strawberries™

INGREDIENTS

Makes 4-6 servings

- 1 cup 8 Oz. (226 g.) Mascarpone cheese (room temperature)
- 3 Eggs
- 4 Tbsp of sugar
- Pinch of salt
- 1 Cup almond milk
- 3 Tbsp of water
- 1 Tbsp of vanilla extract
- 4 Tbsp of cocoa powder
- 20 Fresh strawberries per person

Ladyfingers Quantity:
Cake Pan (9x9) : 24 (12 for layers)
Glasses and Bowls: 2-4 for glass (1-2 for layers)

Download Shopping list

DIRECTIONS

How to make a basic cream

1. **With** an electric mixer, beat the egg whites until stiff. Add a pinch of salt and 1 Tbsp of sugar while mixing
2. **In** a separate bowl, beat the egg yolks, adding 3 Tbsp of sugar. Beat until the mixture has a consistency of mousse (about 3-4 minutes)
3. **Add** the mascarpone cheese to the egg yolk mixture. Beat quickly at a reduced speed until creamy. Using a wooden spoon, fold in the egg whites

How to make a vanilla cream

4. **Divide** the basic cream in two parts (place the cream in two seprate bowls)
5. **In** one bowl add 1 Tbsp of vanilla extract in to the cream ("Vanilla cream")
6. **Gently** mix with a spoon

How to make a chocolate cream

7. **In** the other bowl add 4 Tbsp of cocoa powder in to the cream ("Chocolate cream")
8. **Gently** mix with a spoon

How to make the tiramisù

9. **In** a separate bowl combine 1 cup Almond milk and 3 Tbsp of water for dipping
10. **Dip** each Ladyfinger into the almond milk for only 2-3 seconds
11. **Fo**r this dessert use one of the following containers: 9x9 cake pan (glass, plastic, ceramic, alluminium): Glasses (8-12 Fl. Oz.): Bowls (8-12 Fl. Oz.) place a layer of the "Vanilla cream" and fresh strawberries then the Ladyfingers soaked in a almond milk and again place a layer of the "Chocolate cream". Repeat for 2 layers.
12. **On top** add the fresh stawberries
13. **Chill** at least 2-3 hours before serving

Link additional content

www.tiramisuamoremio.com/tiramisu-vanilla-chocolate-strawberry

Tiramisu Amore Mio

Coconut Tiramisù™

INGREDIENTS

Makes 4-6 servings

- 1 Cup 8 Oz. (226 g.) Mascarpone cheese (room temperature)
- 3 Eggs
- 4 Tbsp of sugar
- Pinch of salt
- 7 Oz. (200 g.) Sponge cake
- 1-2 Cups of shredded coconut
- 1 Tbsp of cocoa podwer
- 1 Tbsp of vanilla extract
- 3 Tbsp of water

Download Shopping list

DIRECTIONS

HOW TO MAKE THE BASIC CREAM

1. **With** an electric mixer, beat the egg whites until stiff. Add a pinch of salt and 1 Tbsp of sugar while mixing
2. **In** a separate bowl, beat the egg yolks, adding 3 Tbsp of sugar. Beat until the mixture has a consistency of mousse (about 3-4 minutes)
3. **Add** the mascarpone cheese to the egg yolk mixture. Beat quickly at a reduced speed until creamy. Using a wooden spoon, fold in the egg whites
4. **Divide** the basic cream in two parts (place the cream in two seprate bowls)

HOW TO MAKE A COCONUT CREAM

5. **Add** the 1/4 cup of coconut powder in one of part of "Basic cream" ("Coconut cream")
6. **Mix** with a spoon (gently)

HOW TO MAKE THE TIRAMISÙ

7. **In** a separate bowl add the vanilla extract and 3 Tbsp of water
8. **Cut** Sponge Cake into vertical slices exactly 1/4 inch thick. You can use the small pieces to fill in any gaps
9. **With** a pastry brush moisten the sponge cake with the vanilla extract
10. **Fo**r this dessert use one of the following containers: 9x9 cake pan (glass, plastic, ceramic, alluminium): Glasses (8 or more Fl. Oz.): Bowls (8-12 Fl. Oz.) place a layer of the "Coconut cream", then the sponge cake soaked in a vanilla and again place a layer of the "Basic cream". Repeat for 2 layers.
11. **Sprinkle** the top with 1 Tbsp of cocoa powder and 1/4 Cup of coconut powder
12. **Chill** at least 2-3 hours before serving

Link additional content

www.tiramisuamoremio.com/tiramisu-coconut

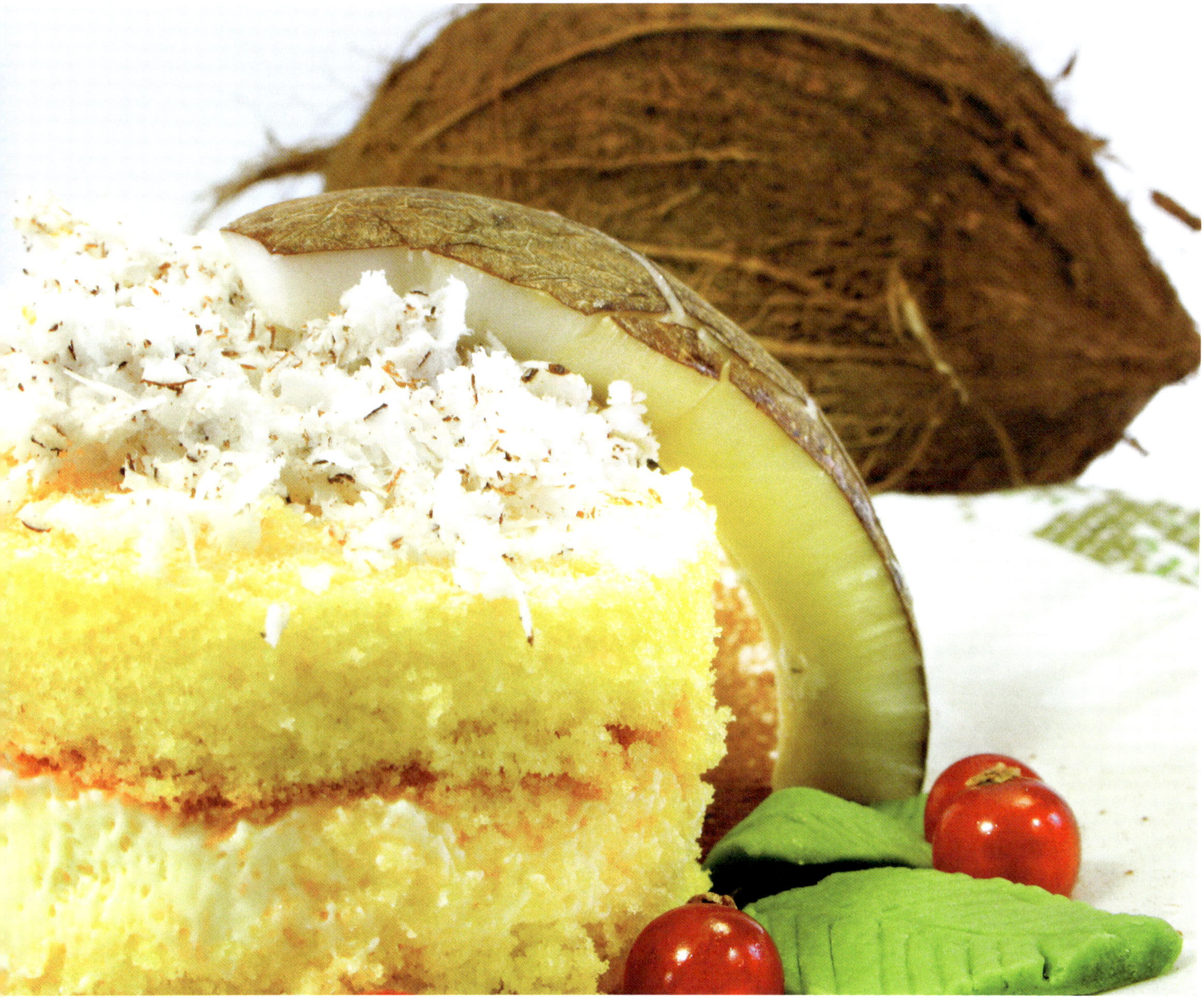

TIRA

RECIPES

FRUITS

MISU

With

Alcohol

Limoncello Tiramisù™

INGREDIENTS

Makes 4-6 servings

- 1 Cup 8 Oz. (226 g.) mascarpone cheese (room temperature)
- 3 eggs
- 4 Tbsp of sugar
- Pinch of salt
- 7 Oz. (200 g.) Sponge Cake
- 2 lemons (Possibly organic)
- 1-2 cups of Limoncello
- Caramel for decoration (optional)

Download Shopping list

DIRECTIONS

For Frozen lemon (time in refrigerator 1-2 hours):

- Cut the lemon into very thin slices (the thinner the better, as these will be added directly to the tiramisù), discarding the seeds
- Line the slices of lemon on a baked paper (non stick) and sprinkle sugar on
- Freeze for least 1/2 hours

how to make the basic cream

1. **With** an electric mixer, beat the egg whites until stiff. Add a pinch of salt and 1 Tbsp of sugar while mixing
2. **In** a separate bowl, beat the egg yolks, adding 3 Tbsp of sugar. Beat until the mixture has a consistency of mousse (about 3-4 minutes)
3. **Add** the mascarpone cheese to the egg yolk mixture. Beat quickly at a reduced speed until creamy. Using a wooden spoon, fold in the egg whites

how to make the tiramisu

4. **In** a separate bowl place the cups of Limoncello for dipping
5. **Cut** Sponge Cake into vertical slices exactly 1/4 inch thick. You can use the small pieces to fill in any gaps
6. **With** a pastry brush moisten the sponge cake with the Limoncello
7. **For** this dessert use one of the following containers: 9x9 cake pan (glass, plastic, ceramic, alluminium): Glasses (8 or more Fl. Oz.): Bowls (8-12 Fl. Oz.) place a layer of the "Basic cream", then the sponge cake soaked in a Limoncello and add the slices of frozen lemon. Repeat for 2 layers.
8. **Add** the caramel on top for decoration
9. **Chill** at least 2-3 hours before serving

Link additional content

www.tiramisuamoremio.com/tiramisu-frozen-lemon-limoncello

Tiramisu Amore Mio

Tiramisù with Dried Fruits and Cointreau™

INGREDIENTS

Makes 4-6 servings
- 1 Cup 8 Oz. (226 g.) mascarpone cheese (room temperature)
- 3 eggs
- 4 Tbsp of sugar
- Pinch of salt
- 7 Oz. (200 g.) Sponge cake
- 10 dried figs cut 1/2" cubes
- 20 dried apricots cut 1/2" cubes
- 1 Cup crystallized ginger (in cubes)
- 1 Tbsp cocoa powder
- 1 cup of Cointreau

Download Shopping list

DIRECTIONS

HOW TO MAKE THE BASIC CREAM

1. **With** an electric mixer, beat the egg whites until stiff. Add a pinch of salt and 1 Tbsp of sugar while mixing.
2. **In** a separate bowl, beat the egg yolks, adding 3 Tbsp of sugar. Beat until the mixture has a consistency of mousse (about 3-4 minutes)
3. **Add** the mascarpone cheese and the dry fruits to the egg yolk mixture. Beat quickly at a reduced speed until creamy. Using a wooden spoon, fold in the egg whites.

HOW TO MAKE THE TIRAMISÙ

4. **In** a separate bowl place a cup of the Cointreau for dipping
5. **Cut** Sponge Cake into vertical slices exactly 1/4 inch thick. You can use the small pieces to fill in any gaps
6. **With** a pastry brush moisten the sponge cake with the Cointreau
7. **For** this dessert use one of the following containers: 9x9 cake pan (glass, plastic, ceramic, alluminium): Glasses (8 or more Fl. Oz.): Bowls (8-12 Fl. Oz.) place a layer of the "Basic cream," dried figs, dried apricots and ginger and then the sponge cake soaked in a Cointreau. Repeat for 2 layers.
8. **Add** on top the Tbsp of cocoa powder and again the figs, apricots and ginger
9. **Chill** at least 2-3 hours before serving

Link additional content

www.tiramisuamoremio.com/tiramisu-dried-fruits-cointreau

Tiramisu Amore Mio

Tiramisù Piña colada™

INGREDIENTS

Makes 4-6 servings
- 1 Cup 8 Oz. (226 g.) Mascarpone cheese (room temperature)
- 3 Eggs
- 6 Tbsp of sugar
- Pinch of salt
- 7 Oz. (200 g.) Sponge cake
- 12 Tbsp of coconut powder
- 14 Oz. (396 g.) Pineapple Chunks (Cans)
- Cup of White Rum
- Lemon juice (2 lemons)

Caramelized pineapple
- 2 Tbsp unsalted butter
- 3 Tbsp packed brown sugar (preferably dark)

Download Shopping list

DIRECTIONS

Caramelized Pineapple:
Cut pineapple into portions about 1/4 inch (0.6 cm) to 3/8 inch (1 cm) wide. In a small saucepan cook butter, 2 Tbsps brown sugar, and rum over moderate heat, stirring, 1 minute. Add pineapple, stirring to coat, and cook mixture 1 minute.
To use wait until room temperature

how to make the basic cream
1. **With** an electric mixer, beat the egg whites until stiff. Add a pinch of salt and 1 Tbsp of sugar while mixing
2. **In** a separate bowl, beat the egg yolks, adding 3 Tbsp of sugar. Beat until the mixture has a consistency of mousse (about 3-4 minutes)
3. **Add** the mascarpone cheese to the egg yolk mixture. Beat quickly at a reduced speed until creamy. Using a wooden spoon, fold in the egg whites

how to make the coconut cream
4. **Add** the 9 Tbsp of coconut powder in a "Basic cream" ("Coconut cream")
5. **Gently** mix with a spoon

how to make the tiramisù
6. **In** a separate bowl place the cup of the white Rum for dipping
7. **Cut** Sponge Cake into vertical slices exactly 1/4 inch thick. You can use the small pieces to fill in any gaps
8. **With** a pastry brush moisten the sponge cake with the white Rum
9. **Fo**r this dessert use one of the following containers: 9x9 cake pan (glass, plastic, ceramic, alluminium): Glasses (8 or more Fl. Oz.): Bowls (8-12 Fl. Oz.) place a layer of the "Coconut cream", then the sponge cake soaked in a Rum and half part of caramelized pineapple. Repeat for 2 layers.
10. **Sprinkle** the top with 3 Tbsp of coconut powder
11. **Chill** at least 2-3 hours before serving

Link additional content

www.tiramisuamoremio.com/tiramisu-pinacolada

Tiramisu Amore Mio

SPECIAL

RECIPES

Tiramisù with Stout Beer™

INGREDIENTS

Makes 4-6 servings

- 1 Cup 8 Oz. (226 g.) mascarpone cheese (room temperature)
- 3 Eggs
- 4 Tbsp of sugar
- Pinch of salt
- 7 Oz. (200 g.) Sponge cake
- 2 Cups stout beer
- 1 Cup 8 Oz. (226 g.) Whipped Heavy cream

DIRECTIONS

HOW TO MAKE THE BASIC CREAM

1. **With** an electric mixer, beat the egg whites until stiff. Add a pinch of salt and 1 Tbsp of sugar while mixing
2. **In** a separate bowl, beat the egg yolks, adding 3 Tbsp of sugar. Beat until the mixture has a consistency of mousse (about 3-4 minutes)
3. **Add** the mascarpone cheese to the egg yolk mixture. Beat quickly at a reduced speed until creamy. Using a wooden spoon, fold in the egg whites

HOW TO MAKE THE TIRAMISÙ

4. **In** a separate bowl place the Stout beer for dipping
5. **Cut** Sponge Cake into vertical slices exactly 1/4 inch thick. You can use the small pieces to fill in any gaps
6. **With** a pastry brush moisten the sponge cake with the beer
7. **With** an eletric mixer, beat the heavy cream until stiff
8. **Fo**r this dessert use one of the following containers: 9x9 cake pan (glass, plastic, ceramic, alluminium): Glasses (8 or more Fl. Oz.): Bowls (8-12 Fl. Oz.) place a layer of the "Basic cream", then the sponge cake soaked in a stout beer. Repeat for 2 layers.
9. **Add** on top the heavy cream (whipped)
10. **Chill** at least 2-3 hours before serving

Download Shopping list

Link additional content

www.tiramisuamoremio.com/tiramisu-stout-beer

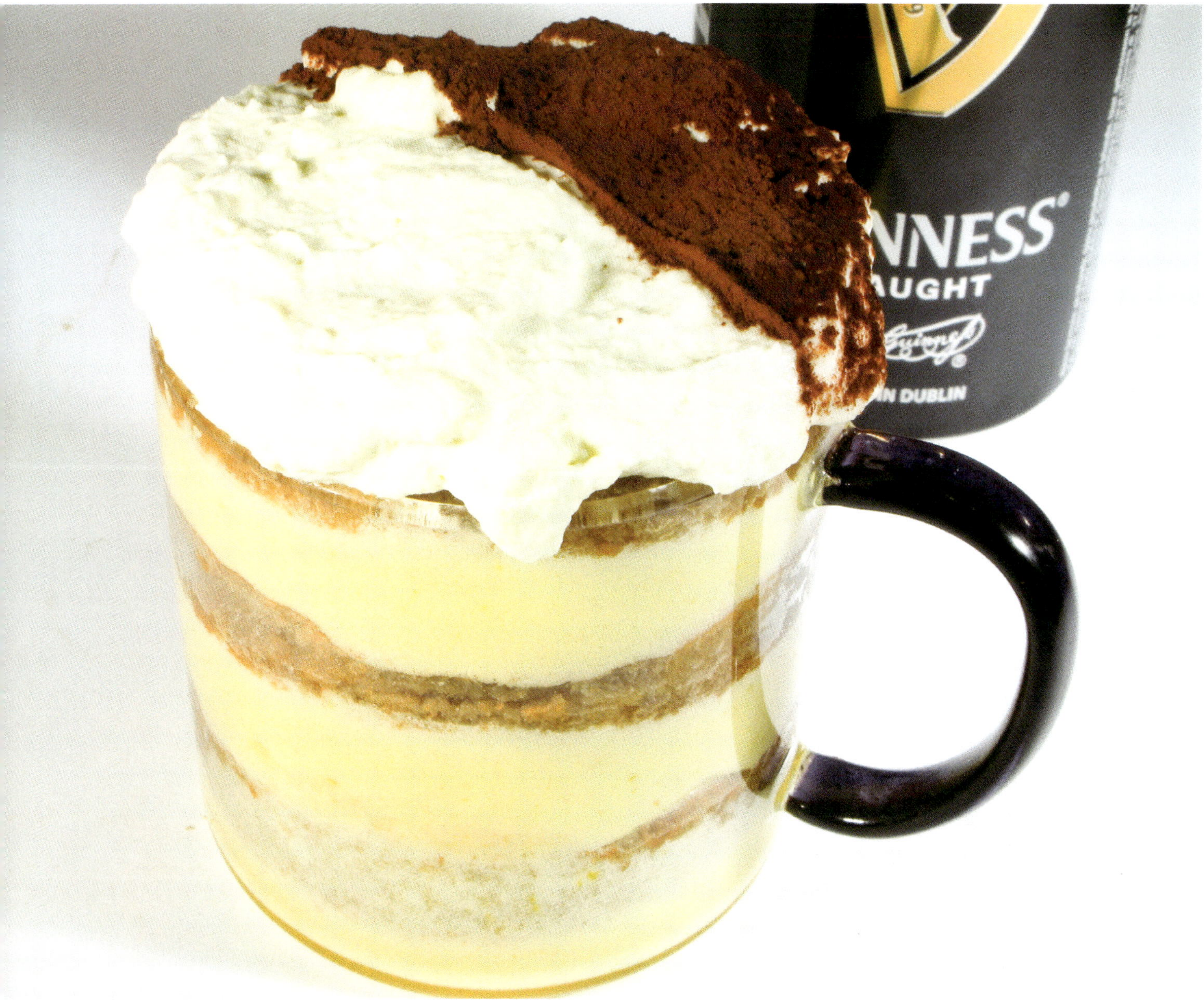

Chocolate and Red Chili Tiramisù™

INGREDIENTS

Makes 4-6 servings
- 1 Cup 8 Oz. (226 g.) Mascarpone cheese (room temperature)
- 3 Eggs
- 4 Tbsp of sugar
- Pinch of salt
- 7 Oz. (200 g.) Sponge cake
- 1 Tbsp of vanilla extract
- 3 Tbsp of water
- 3 Tbsp of cocoa powder
- 1 Tbsp of chili powder

Download Shopping list

DIRECTIONS

HOW TO MAKE THE BASIC CREAM

1. **With** an electric mixer, beat the egg whites until stiff. Add a pinch of salt and 1 Tbsp of sugar while mixing
2. **In** a separate bowl, beat the egg yolks, adding 3 Tbsp of sugar. Beat until the mixture has a consistency of mousse (about 3-4 minutes)
3. **Add** the mascarpone cheese to the egg yolk mixture. Beat quickly at a reduced speed until creamy. Using a wooden spoon, fold in the egg whites

HOW TO MAKE THE CHOCOLATE AND CHILI CREAM

4. **Add** 4 Tbsp of cocoa powder and chili powder in to the "Basic cream" ("Chocolate and Chili cream")
5. **Gently** mix with a spoon

HOW TO MAKE THE TIRAMISÙ

6. **In** a separate bowl combine a Tbsp of vanilla extract and 3 Tbsp of water
7. **Cut** Sponge Cake into vertical slices exactly 1/4 inch thick. You can use the small pieces to fill in any gaps
8. **With** a pastry brush moisten the sponge cake with the vanilla extract
9. **Fo**r this dessert use one of the following containers: 9x9 cake pan (glass, plastic, ceramic, alluminium): Glasses (8 or more Fl. Oz.): Bowls (8-12 Fl. Oz.) place a layer of the "Chocolate and Chili cream" then the sponge cake soaked in a vanilla extract. Repeat for 2 layers.
10. **Sprinkle** the top with cocoa powder
11. **Chill** at least 2-3 hours before serving

Link additional content

www.tiramisuamoremio.com/tiramisu-chocolate-chili

Tiramisu Amore Mio

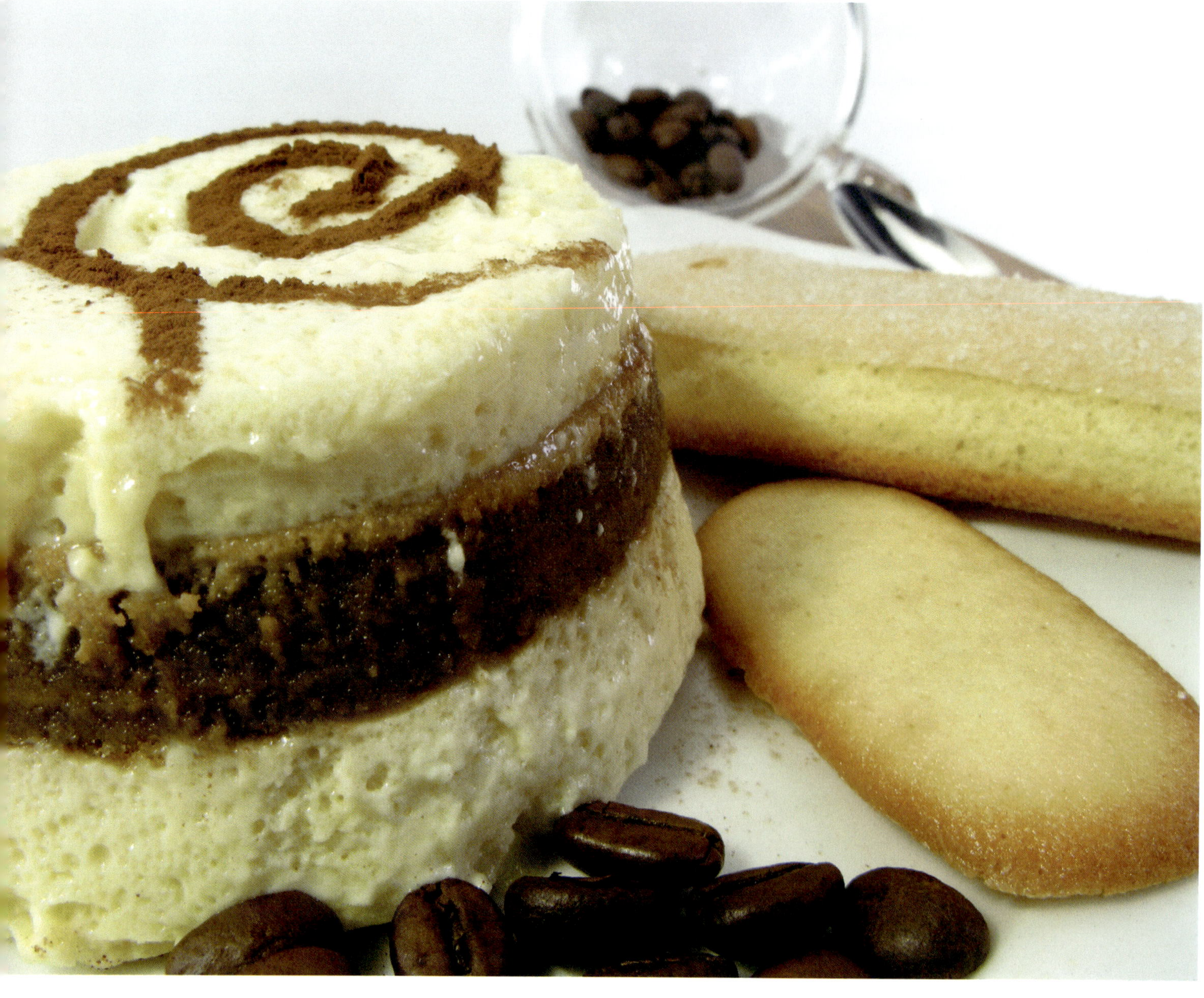

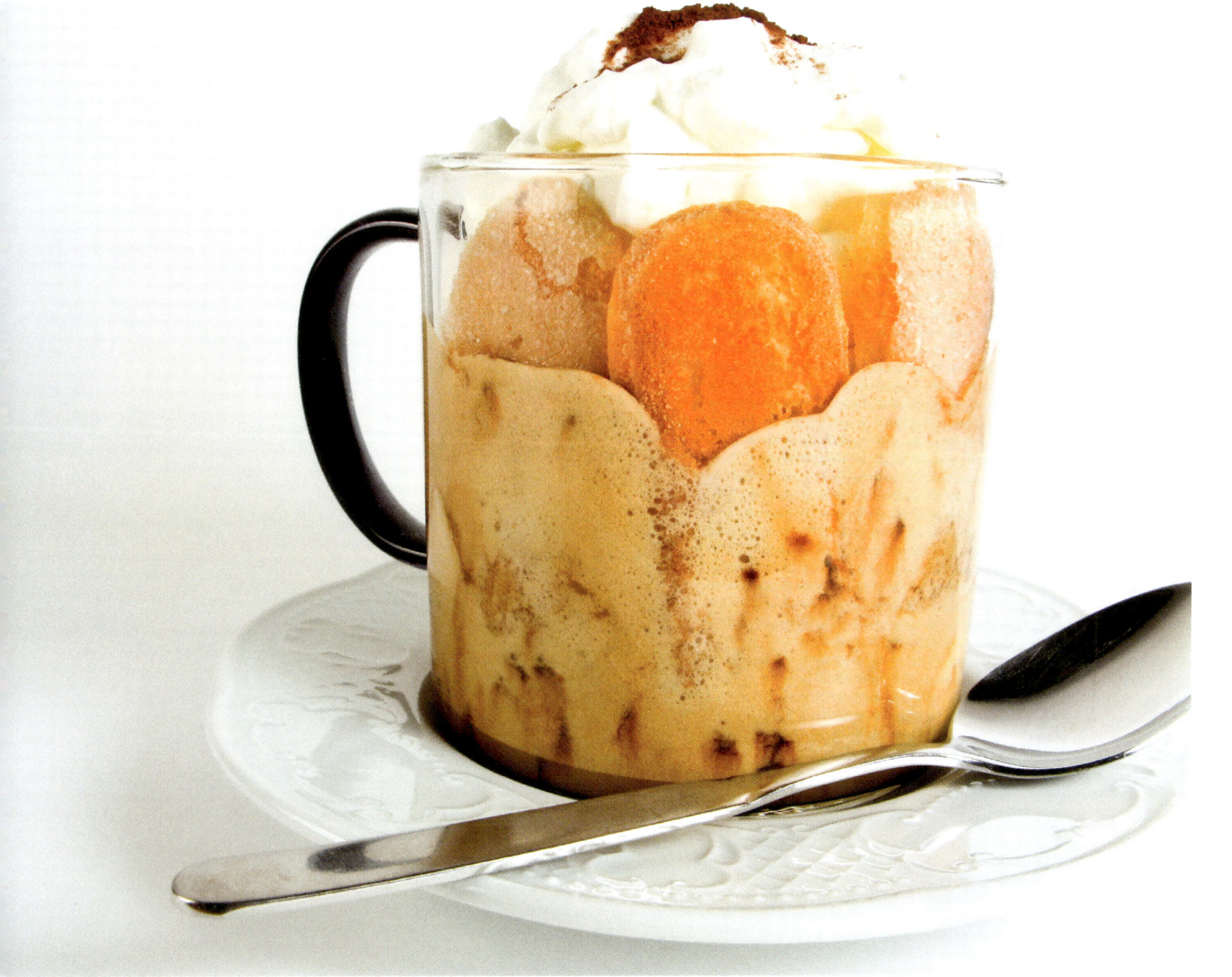

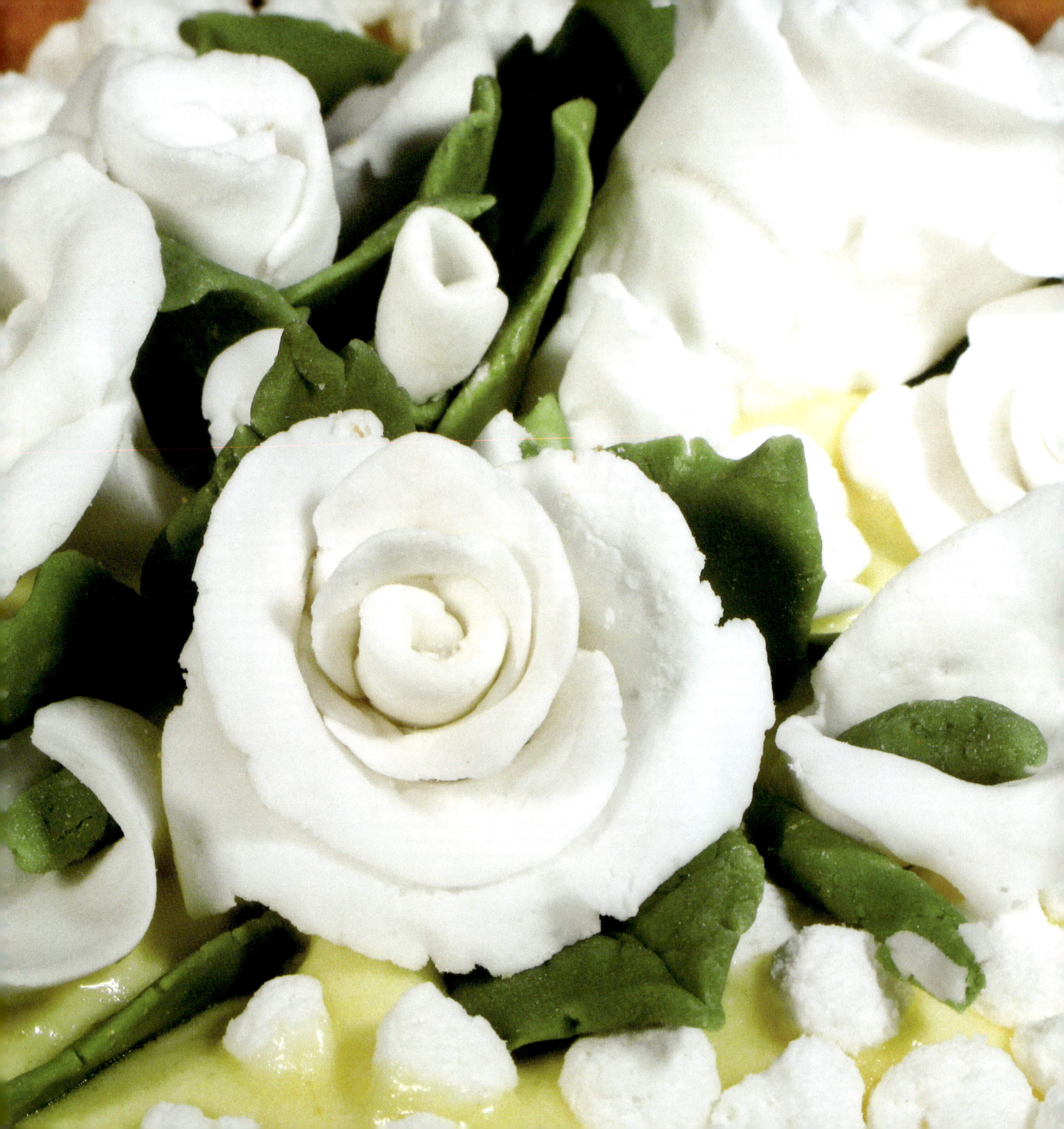

CPSIA information can be obtained
at www.ICGtesting.com
Printed in the USA
LVIC04n2333060714
393071LV00009B/201